OPPOSING VIEWPOINTS® SERIES

Debt

Other Books of Related Interest:

Opposing Viewpoints Series

Consumerism

The Federal Budget

The Middle Class

White Collar Crime

Current Controversies Series

Capitalism

Consumer Debt

The Global Economy

The U.S. Economy

At Issue Series

Does Outsourcing Harm America?

Should the Federal Government Bail Out Private Industry?

Teens and Credit

"Congress shall make no law . . . abridging the freedom of speech, or of the press."

First Amendment to the U.S. Constitution

The basic foundation of our democracy is the First Amendment guarantee of freedom of expression. The Opposing Viewpoints Series is dedicated to the concept of this basic freedom and the idea that it is more important to practice it than to enshrine it.

Debt

Christina Fisanick, Book Editor

GREENHAVEN PRESS
A part of Gale, Cengage Learning

GALE
CENGAGE Learning™

Detroit • New York • San Francisco • New Haven, Conn • Waterville, Maine • London

Christine Nasso, *Publisher*
Elizabeth Des Chenes, *Managing Editor*

© 2010 Greenhaven Press, a part of Gale, Cengage Learning.

Gale and Greenhaven Press are registered trademarks used herein under license.

For more information, contact:
Greenhaven Press
27500 Drake Rd.
Farmington Hills, MI 48331-3535
Or you can visit our Internet site at gale.cengage.com

For product information and technology assistance, contact us at

Gale Customer Support, 1-800-877-4253
For permission to use material from this text or product, submit all requests online at www.cengage.com/permissions

Further permissions questions can be emailed to permissionrequest@cengage.com

Articles in Greenhaven Press anthologies are often edited for length to meet page requirements. In addition, original titles of these works are changed to clearly present the main thesis and to explicitly indicate the author's opinion. Every effort is made to ensure that Greenhaven Press accurately reflects the original intent of the authors. Every effort has been made to trace the owners of copyrighted material.

Cover image © Tom Grill/Photographer's Choice/Getty Images.

LIBRARY OF CONGRESS CATALOGING-IN-PUBLICATION DATA

Debt / Christina Fisanick, book editor.
    p. cm. -- (Opposing viewpoints)
    Includes bibliographical references and index.
    978-0-7377-4202-2 (hbk.)
    978-0-7377-4203-9 (pbk.)
    1. Consumer credit--United States--Juvenile literature. 2. Debt--United States--Juvenile literature. I. Fisanick, Christina.
    HG3756.U54D43 2010
    332.024'02--dc22

                                               2009027494

Printed in the United States of America
1 2 3 4 5 6 7 13 12 11 10 09

Contents

Chapter Three: Does the U.S. Government Manage Debt Responsibly?

Why Consider Opposing Viewpoints?

> *"The only way in which a human being can make some approach to knowing the whole of a subject is by hearing what can be said about it by persons of every variety of opinion and studying all modes in which it can be looked at by every character of mind. No wise man ever acquired his wisdom in any mode but this."*
>
> *John Stuart Mill*

In our media-intensive culture it is not difficult to find differing opinions. Thousands of newspapers and magazines and dozens of radio and television talk shows resound with differing points of view. The difficulty lies in deciding which opinion to agree with and which "experts" seem the most credible. The more inundated we become with differing opinions and claims, the more essential it is to hone critical reading and thinking skills to evaluate these ideas. Opposing Viewpoints books address this problem directly by presenting stimulating debates that can be used to enhance and teach these skills. The varied opinions contained in each book examine many different aspects of a single issue. While examining these conveniently edited opposing views, readers can develop critical thinking skills such as the ability to compare and contrast authors' credibility, facts, argumentation styles, use of persuasive techniques, and other stylistic tools. In short, the Opposing Viewpoints Series is an ideal way to attain the higher-level thinking and reading skills so essential in a culture of diverse and contradictory opinions.

In addition to providing a tool for critical thinking, Opposing Viewpoints books challenge readers to question their own strongly held opinions and assumptions. Most people form their opinions on the basis of upbringing, peer pressure, and personal, cultural, or professional bias. By reading carefully balanced opposing views, readers must directly confront new ideas as well as the opinions of those with whom they disagree. This is not to simplistically argue that everyone who reads opposing views will—or should—change his or her opinion. Instead, the series enhances readers' understanding of their own views by encouraging confrontation with opposing ideas. Careful examination of others' views can lead to the readers' understanding of the logical inconsistencies in their own opinions, perspective on why they hold an opinion, and the consideration of the possibility that their opinion requires further evaluation.

Evaluating Other Opinions

To ensure that this type of examination occurs, Opposing Viewpoints books present all types of opinions. Prominent spokespeople on different sides of each issue as well as well-known professionals from many disciplines challenge the reader. An additional goal of the series is to provide a forum for other, less known, or even unpopular viewpoints. The opinion of an ordinary person who has had to make the decision to cut off life support from a terminally ill relative, for example, may be just as valuable and provide just as much insight as a medical ethicist's professional opinion. The editors have two additional purposes in including these less known views. One, the editors encourage readers to respect others' opinions—even when not enhanced by professional credibility. It is only by reading or listening to and objectively evaluating others' ideas that one can determine whether they are worthy of consideration. Two, the inclusion of such viewpoints encourages the important critical thinking skill of objectively evaluating an author's credentials and bias. This evaluation will illuminate an author's reasons for taking a particular stance on an issue and will aid in readers' evaluation of the author's ideas.

It is our hope that these books will give readers a deeper understanding of the issues debated and an appreciation of the complexity of even seemingly simple issues when good and honest people disagree. This awareness is particularly important in a democratic society such as ours in which people enter into public debate to determine the common good. Those with whom one disagrees should not be regarded as enemies but rather as people whose views deserve careful examination and may shed light on one's own.

Thomas Jefferson once said that "difference of opinion leads to inquiry, and inquiry to truth." Jefferson, a broadly educated man, argued that "if a nation expects to be ignorant and free . . . it expects what never was and never will be." As individuals and as a nation, it is imperative that we consider the opinions of others and examine them with skill and discernment. The Opposing Viewpoints Series is intended to help readers achieve this goal.

David L. Bender and Bruno Leone,
Founders

Introduction

"When you get prices increasing faster than the underlying costs, sometimes there can be pretty serious consequences."

—Investor Warren Buffett, on the housing market bubble, in 2006

When the housing bubble burst in 2007, few industry insiders were surprised. Like similar markets that are based on the success and failure of other industries, the housing market had suffered highs and lows in the past. What wasn't expected was the catastrophic toll the housing bust took on the national economy. The fall of the housing market signaled the beginning of an economic recession that has been compared to the Great Depression of the 1930s. No one would deny that the United States is in difficult financial straits, but identifying who is responsible for the housing bust and subsequent economic downturn remains up for debate.

As housing prices soared in the late 1990s and early 2000s, lenders began to tighten their lending practices, requiring larger down payments and higher credit scores from borrowers. Unfortunately, these new restrictions made it even harder for low-income and middle-class families to afford their own homes. To remedy this situation, lenders began using adjustable rate mortgages (ARMs) as a way for potential borrowers to afford homes that would normally be beyond their means. Most borrowers who opt for an ARM usually have the intention of refinancing or even selling their home before the mortgage rate goes up. According to Keith Gumbinger of HSH Associates, "Many low-income and first-time home buyers [opted] for adjustable rate mortgages because they [couldn't] afford a fixed-rate mortgage."

The problem with ARMs is that payments change as interest rates change. The Federal Reserve Board notes in *Consumer Handbook on Adjustable Rate Mortgages*, "Payment shock may occur if your mortgage payment rises sharply at a rate adjustment." An interest rate increase of just 1 percent can make a dramatic difference in a mortgage payment. These payment shocks led to many foreclosures, which contributed to the housing bust. According to a 2008 report by the Mortgage Bankers Association, "Nearly 12 percent of all Americans with a mortgage—a record 5.4 million homeowners—were at least one month late or in foreclosure at the end of last year." Few Americans can forget the news reports of borrowers being forced from their homes because of foreclosure.

Economic pundits claim that lenders sought to make a profit no matter the future consequences. According to a May 2008 article in *The Atlantic* by John Ritter, "Predatory lenders did bamboozle some people into loans and houses they couldn't afford." Other analysts claim that the blame is more wide reaching than lenders. In a May 20, 2009, interview with *Reason*, economist Thomas Sowell argues, "The people I would blame the most . . . are the politicians—people in Congress and the president and regulators—who pushed the lenders and the banks and Fannie Mae and Freddie Mac into lending and buying mortgages based on people who didn't meet standards that evolved in the marketplace and which had worked." He asserts that the government ignored warnings from research organizations that such lending practices would lead to crisis.

Other analysts argue that the housing bust and the subsequent economic disaster are the result of poor choices made by borrowers who knowingly went in over their heads. Some homebuyers found themselves able to buy homes that they previously could not afford, and when faced with such an option, many borrowers ignored future rate changes and payment shocks. In a December 2007 interview with Diana Olick of *Consumers Digest*, Guy Cecala, publisher of *Inside Mortgage Finance*, said "Somebody who maybe should have been shopping for a two hundred thousand dollar home ended up buying a four hundred thousand dollar or five hundred thousand [dollar] home because they had artificially low interest payments." In the end, however, rates went up and so did mortgage payments.

Whether the housing bust was due to adjustable rate mortgages or the practices of lenders, politicians, and borrowers remains up for debate. Some critics argue that understanding the roots of the global economic crisis is key to preventing such catastrophe in the future. The authors in *Opposing Viewpoints: Debt* debate current views on debt in the following chapters: "What Are Some Attitudes Toward Debt?" "Do Some People Struggle to Manage Debt Responsibly?" "Does the U.S. Government Manage Debt Responsibly?" and "How Can Debt Problems Be Solved?"

CHAPTER 1

What Are Some Attitudes Toward Debt?

Chapter Preface

By investigating prior debt obligations, credit scoring companies such as TransUnion, Experian, and others develop a score that reflects the consumer's likelihood of loan repayment, known as a FICO score (FICO stands for Fair Isaac Corporation, the name of the company that originally developed the scoring system). FICO scores run between 300 on the low end to 850 at the top. According to institutions that use this score as a determining factor, the higher a consumer's score, the more likely that person will pay off his or her debts. In the last several years, controversy has erupted regarding the use of FICO scores in situations not directly related to lending, including hiring and promoting employees and phone and utility service installation. The use of credit scores in determining whether or not a person can acquire auto and home insurance and what rate he or she will pay has consumer watchdogs and customers speaking out.

Insurance companies have been using credit scores to determine rates since the mid-1990s, arguing that a person's credit score is directly related to the number of claims that he or she will file. In 2003 the Federal Trade Commission (FTC) was directed by the Fair and Accurate Credit Transactions Act (FACTA) to assess whether there is a relationship between credit score and insurance claims filed. The FTC's final report, published in 2007, reveals that there is indeed a correlation. According to the report, "Scores effectively predict the number of claims consumers file and the total costs of those claims." In other words, the lower the score, the higher the number and cost of claims filed. Therefore, insurance companies justify the use of credit scores in determining credit rates by arguing that customers who will likely file fewer claims should pay lower rates.

Not everyone agrees with this assumption, including Pamela Jones Harbour, one of the commissioners who worked on the FTC report. She argues that the methodology used to generate the report was flawed because the data depended "solely on two sources of information: data the insurance industry was willing to turn over voluntarily, and data that were publicly available." She insists that better sources for data were available. Her dissenting statement has been used by consumer advocates, including the Consumer Federation of America, the National Fair Housing Alliance, the National Consumer Law Center, and the Center for Economic and Social Justice, who have been arguing for many years about the injustice of basing insurance rates on credit scores. In a response to the FTC's report, Norma Garcia, senior staff attorney with Consumers Union, states, "Insurance premiums should be based on the risk of an accident, not a consumer's bill paying record for other goods and services."

Credit scores were originally formulated as a means of determining a borrower's probability of repaying a loan, a figure once calculated in part by a lender's personal relationship with a customer. As lending companies grow in number and in size, they will increasingly rely on impersonal data to evaluate a potential borrower's risk. The same is true of insurance companies. They have little else to use in determining a motorist's or home owner's risk of filing a claim. Much like the authors in the following chapter debate, attitudes about credit and how it can be managed responsibly will continue to play an important role in the economic landscape.

> *"Much like cholesterol, where there is good and bad cholesterol, debt comes in two versions."*

Going into Debt Can Be a Good Financial Choice

Tom Allen

Tom Allen is a contributor to financial Web sites, including IHateDebt.com, from which the following viewpoint is excerpted. He argues that going into debt is often not the wisest choice, especially if the borrower is using money on unnecessary purchases. He insists, however, that in cases of emergencies and long-term investments, taking on debt might be unavoidable and even a solid financial decision. Allen encourages potential borrowers to consider going into debt carefully and to try and find alternative routes to paying for life's expenses.

As you read, consider the following questions:

1. What are the two most common unexpected events that cause people to go into debt?

2. What are three good reasons for going into debt?

3. What is the difference between a sole proprietorship and a corporation?

How many times a day do you see a credit card logo on a cash register? Why do they still call them cash registers when they really want you to charge anyway? How much is spent in advertising to get you to spend what you don't have just because you have room left on your credit card? Maybe you thought that sale was just too good to pass up. Maybe you thought that you could handle the payments and maybe you could until ... late fees, over-the-limit fees, the increase of your interest rate, you got sick for a week or maybe there was even a real emergency.

Getting into debt is easy, just buy a few things that you can't afford to pay cash for and don't think about how many payments you're going to have to make before it's paid off completely. Getting into debt is fun; just go out to dinner and a show or away for a few days to make yourself feel better about the fact that you don't have the money to go out to dinner and a show or to get away for a few days. Getting into debt can impress people. Don't drive around in something that you can afford to pay for, figure out how much you can squeeze out of your monthly budget, and if you don't have a budget, even better just guess, then tell a car salesperson that you'd like to make 48 payments and see what you'll be driving around town in. The best part is you'll guarantee you'll be driving it to work for the next 1,460 days just to make the payments. Now that's impressive!

Take the "How Did I Get Into Debt Quiz." Pull out one of your credit cards and determine how much you owe on it. Now, quickly, what did you buy for all that money? I'll bet you don't know because you bought stuff. Stuff you may not even have anymore let alone still use or be able to identify. Now ask why do you use it at all? Be honest. How does "I want stuff I can't afford to pay cash for" sound?

The Unexpected Event

Many people get into debt because of unexpected events, events beyond their control. The most common of these are medical bills and job loss. And the most common causes are lack of affordable medical insurance and globalization. Not only are these problems beyond your control, they also appear to be beyond the control of our political system so don't expect the problems to be fixed any time soon.

Globalization, the process of businesses taking their money to far off countries to earn better returns, is not new. In the 1790s Benjamin Franklin Bache [grandson of Benjamin Franklin] published a newspaper called the *Aurora*. In it he wrote that he believed that the merchants of the day were "men who know no country but that where they can make money," who "carry their capitals ships and our sailors to the country which will encourage them."

The sad part, debt-wise, of having an unexpected event is that even though you didn't cause the problem it is up to you to fix it. So whether you're in debt because of an event or the "easy monthly payments" trap relax because I've got some good news. Getting out of debt is going to be even more fun than getting into debt was. I've done both and becoming debt-free feels great. So if you're ready let's get started . . . but first let's discuss, Good Debt/Bad Debt and business debt.

Good Debt/Bad Debt

Much like cholesterol, where there is good and bad cholesterol, debt comes in two versions. It can be okay to take on debt in a reasoned way for a good purpose. In fact many people become wealthy by borrowing money to invest in business opportunities. They call it using other people's money. But my focus here is on how individuals spend their money on themselves. It's how you spend your money.

There can be some very good reasons to take on debt. Financing education, for example, can be an admirable thing. If you go to school to increase your income potential, taking out a student loan would be a good thing. If you take out a $2,000 loan and you learn a skill that lets you earn an extra $5,000 a year, you'd be crazy not to take the loan. If you take out a student loan because you don't know what you want to do with your life and you don't want to get a job, well, that's not a good idea.

For most people taking out a mortgage is the only way they'll be able to purchase a home. This could be considered good debt. Because of the way mortgage payments are structured with the first few years being heavily weighted towards paying interest and mere pittance going towards principal, it's a good idea to pay off even this good debt as soon as possible. Many wise financial minds teach that before investing in something that will give you thirty years of monthly payments it's better to invest in income producing assets first, something like rental property.

Well, what about if there's an emergency? Maybe the plumbing broke, or you have a medical emergency. Well let's not be stupid about this, if it's a real emergency and the only way to pay for it is by taking on debt, then take it on. If you break your leg it's a good idea to take on the debt of a doctor's bill rather then waiting until you have the money to get the bone set.

Personal vs. Business Debt

There can be some big differences between personal and business debt. But it mostly depends upon how the business structure is set up. If the business is set up as a sole-proprietorship then there really is no difference between the business owner and the business, it is all considered one entity.

If on the other hand the business is set up as a corporation then there is a vast difference between the business and the business owner, in this case the shareholders. This is true even if only one person owns all the shares. Legally the corpo-

Secured Credit Cards Can Help Build Credit

Secured credit cards are similar to regular credit cards in that they carry comparable interest rates, annual fees and must be paid every month. However, unlike your standard-issue Visa or MasterCard, the secured card is backed by a deposit from the borrower, which can range from as little as $200 to as much as $10,000.

The amount of your deposit doubles as your line of credit. That's why the card is called "secured." So, if you put $1,000 into a secured account with your lender and then go out and buy a 42-inch Panasonic plasma-screen television for $899.99 at your local Costco, you'll only have a $100.01 credit line. Moreover, you'll have to make at least the minimum payment on the purchase every month.

Carl Winfield,
"Secured Credit Cards Can Help Build Credit,"
Mainstreet.com, March 23, 2009.

ration is considered a separate entity and if the business has debt problems it doesn't translate to shareholder debt problems. That's why entrepreneurs like having their businesses in a separate legal entity.

It's also why if you are considering going into business as a way to make more money to get out of debt it's a good idea to have the proper business structure.

Is There Another Way?

Even with good debt you want to think twice before taking it on. Taking a student loan to improve your employment situation is a great idea, good debt. But wait, before you take on debt ask "Is there a better way?" There are many sources of grants, and yes a grant is money that you don't have to pay back. So before you take the easy way and "Just sign here," do some checking to make sure there's not a better way. You need to be fully informed as to the terms and conditions of any loan before you take it. You should always shop around to see if there is a better deal, better terms or a way to avoid taking the loan out at all.

One way to avoid having to take on even good debt is to plan in advance and save money on a regular basis. If you've been driving for a while you have probably had a flat tire. Because everyone gets a flat tire once in a while it couldn't really be considered an unexpected expense. Do you have money set aside for your next flat tire? Well, you should. If fact you should have money set aside that would cover a variety of "unexpected" expenses. If you do you can deal with life's little surprises without upsetting your monthly budget. You will have to pay yourself back but you won't be charging yourself interest or calling yourself at dinner demanding payment.

So yes, there is good debt under certain conditions, just be sure that you've investigated other ways of taking care of it before you sign your way into debt. And if you do take it on don't allow yourself to feel burdened by it. You did what you had to and you'll pay it off.

| "Not setting up a household budget is how many people got into financial trouble in the first place."

Going into Debt Is a Bad Financial Choice

USA Today (Magazine)

USA Today (Magazine) is published monthly by the Society for the Advancement of Education. In the following viewpoint, Mark Johannessen, the president of the Financial Planning Association in Denver, Colorado, claims that the economic stimulus package does not work. Because many of the consumers are in debt, spending the rebate is not a good option, but if the rebate is not spent, then there is no economic stimulus. He argues that the stimulus will only provide a short-term fix and ultimately encourages consumers to spend more money and go into more debt.

As you read, consider the following questions:

1. According to Mark Johannessen, what is the problem with the rebate approach?

2. When was the last time America had a negative savings rate for a year?

USA Today (Magazine), "Economic Stimulus Carries Wrong Signal," March 2008.

When Is It Worth Going into Debt?

The short answer: It's usually not. When you're in debt, you limit your options and you have less control over your money and your future. You're forking over interest to the bank or credit-card company instead of investing the money in yourself. And especially when you're young, that forces you to lose out on some hefty long-term rewards.

Even in today's tighter financial market, credit comes easy, making it tough to discipline yourself against going into debt. Temptations are everywhere. But just because the loan officer tells you that you can afford the payback terms doesn't mean it's a good idea. It sounds plain and simple, but the sooner you adopt this mindset the better: If you don't have the money, don't buy it.

Erin Burt,
"When Is It Worth Going into Debt?"
Kiplinger.com, July 10, 2008.

3. Instead of encouraging consumers to spend the rebate on unnecessary wants, what does Johannessen desire consumers to do with their rebate?

"It's strangely ironic that Washington is telling Americans to go out and spend to help save our troubled economy," notes Mark Johannessen, president of the Financial Planning Association, Denver, Colo. "It might help the economy, but it won't help Americans dig out of their own spending debt."

Johannessen was reacting to the economic stimulus package that will give citizens an individual rebate of several hundred dollars.

Ecomonic Stimulus Not in Consumer's Best Interest

"The problem with this rebate approach is that it is antisavings and antidebt reductions," he points out. "If individuals do not spend the money, there's no economic stimulus—but the problem is that the average U.S. household credit card debt is [rising sharply]; the national savings rate is [shrinking drastically]; and bankruptcies are on the increase. So, spending the rebate may not be in the best interest of many consumers. Not setting up a household budget is how many people got into financial trouble in the first place."

"American consumers are nearing the one trillion dollar mark in debt for credit cards, mortgages, and other types of loans, and that's truly frightening. The last time we had a negative savings rate for an entire year was 1933 during the Great Depression." Once the checks are in the mail, Johannessen is urging people to consider carefully using the money to pay down their credit card debt or add it to their savings for an emergency fund or retirement. "The subprime mortgage crisis has yet to bottom out and many economists think this stimulus package will provide, at best, a short-term fix, so people may really wish they had that money a few months from now," he contends.

| "Consumers have to recognize the warn-
ing signs of debt."

It Is Possible to Live Debt Free

Leslie E. Royale

Leslie E. Royale is a contributor to Black Enterprise, *a magazine that provides business news and is an investment resource for African Americans. In the following viewpoint, Royale recounts stories of specific citizens in debt and provides examples of how to pull oneself out of debt. Royale claims that while living debt free may seem impossible, all one needs is to recognize specific debt traps.*

As you read, consider the following questions:

1. According to the article, family debt increased by what percent since 1995?

2. What are the common "debt traps?"

3. What five steps can one take in order to get out of debt?

When Suzette Scarborough graduated from Cornell University in 1989, she had 19 different credit cards but was only $5,000 in debt. Immediately upon graduation, she

Leslie E. Royale, "Debt Free Is the Way to Be," *Black Enterprise*, October 2000.

landed a great job with Coopers & Lybrand, in New York, as a human resources professional and was living the life, or so she thought. She would frequently jet across the country with her sorority sisters to various conventions. Developing a taste for the finer things in life, she began to purchase Liz Claiborne suits and Coach bags from Lord & Taylor. She caught all of the Broadway shows, and would travel to different cities just to see Phyllis Hyman sing. Her credit card debt was rising steadily.

Falling into Debt

"I had the mind-set that I didn't have to wait for what I wanted. I could have it now," recalls Scarborough, 33, who resides in Brooklyn, New York. "By 1997, I was $32,000 in debt, including the $10,000 balance on my GEO Prism. I was making all of this money, but it was going to all of these banks."

Scarborough is not alone. According to a Federal Reserve report for May 2000, total consumer debt—mortgages were not factored in—hit $1.45 trillion, up almost 10% from a year ago. The same source reports that credit card debt was $626 million in May 2000, up 8.9% over the previous month. According to Myvesta.org (formerly Debt Counselors of America), an online credit-counseling service, for every dollar the American family earns, it spends $1.22. Family debt was $33,300 in 1998, up 42% from 1995. However, the average net income per family was only $27,219.

Pulling Yourself out of Debt

Determined not to remain a part of these statistics, Scarborough cut up her charge cards and began to track her balances, including how much she was paying off and how much she was accumulating. She read all of the finance articles she could get her hands on, started attending seminars, and began paying down her debt.

By 1999, she owed $25,000. Later that year, she received a $26,500 severance package from her employer. This allowed her to pay off the remaining $22,000.

For many Americans, being debt free may seem like a pipe dream. But it is possible to live a debt-free life. Just know how to recognize the types of debt. In her book *Debt-Proof Living: The Complete Guide to Living Financially Free*, Mary Hunt cites the following "debt traps": credit card accounts, monthly installment plans, overdraft protection plans, past taxes, student loans, medical and dental bills, and personal loans.

"People often find themselves getting into secured debt, such as mortgage and car loans, which they can sell to get out of debt," says Hunt. "But the dangerous types are unsecured debts such as credit cards and signature loans."

According to Michael Kidwell, co-founder of Myvesta.org, consumers have to recognize the warning signs of debt. Those clues may include always having to use credit cards when you make a purchase; only being able to make the minimum payment on cards; and going from using one credit card to using two, three, four, and then five, and never paying off the balances.

In this article we will focus on the elementary methods you can use to get out of debt. In their book *Get Out of Debt: Smart Solutions to Your Money Problems*, authors Kidwell and Steve Rhode, who co-founded Myvesta.org with Kidwell, offer consumers five simple ways to get out of debt: (1) stop incurring debt; (2) track your cash; (3) plan for the future; (4) don't expect instant miracles; and (5) seek professional help. We look at each of these and show you how you can apply them to your financial plan.

Stop Incurring Debt

This keeps you from going further into debt. "Going into debt rarely happens overnight. It usually creeps up over a period of time," says Kidwell. "It starts out innocently with one credit card. Then a large home mortgage, vacations, and student loans. Before we know it, we are living from month-to-month and paycheck-to-paycheck."

Tony and Triscilla Weaver of Stone Mountain, Georgia, know the feeling of living from paycheck to paycheck. Both were raised in single-parent, female-led households where money was always an issue and being debt free was a fantasy. "It showed us both things that we knew we would not want to go through," says Triscilla, 33. "We decided, early on in planning our future together, that we would be debt free."

When the couple married in 1986, their debt consisted of a new $60,000 home, two car loans (Triscilla's monthly payment was $300 and Tony's, $350), and six credit cards between them that included Zales Jewelers, Kay's Jewelers, Goodyear, J.C. Penney, and two separate Rich's Department Store cards. Although Triscilla's charge cards did not carry any balances, Tony's cards, combined, carried a balance of several hundred dollars.

"We sat down with our bills and made a budget. At that time, Tony was making nearly $30,000 per year and I was making less than $15,000," recalls Triscilla. "We decided to pay off all of his credit cards first, and that left us with the two car notes and our house note. It was an uncomfortable feeling having to pay two car notes at the same time, and we said that after that, we would never do it again."

Over the past 14 years, Tony, 37, and Triscilla have alternated getting new cars. She now drives a 1992 Toyota Camry that was paid off in 1995. Tony's 1996 Ford Explorer was paid off this September. During their marriage, they have remained virtually debt free. Their yearly income has more than doubled. As a route manager for the *Atlanta Journal and Constitution*, where he has been employed for 18 years, his salary is $55,000. Triscilla makes $55,000 as the assistant principal of Stephenson Middle School in Stone Mountain.

Develop a Good Debt Strategy

The new motto: The less debt you have, the happier—and wealthier—you'll be. And while even the caviar and Cristal crowd seldom live their whole lives without borrowing, keeping your debt load as light and as cheap as possible is the key to a more secure future and to guilt-free spending on the things you need and want.

It's a skill that's often neglected and seldom discussed, but understanding how to manage your debt will let you build wealth faster, and with less risk. Disciplined saving and smart investing are the topics that get the most ink—hey, we read this magazine too—but without a good debt strategy, the planning for your financial future can get awfully wobbly. The explanation comes down to Home Economics 101: Paying interest works against you in the same way that earning it works for you when you invest. The average household owes about $9,900 on credit cards at an annual rate of 15%, according to the research firm CardTrak.com, costing about $1,500 a year in interest. If a family invested that interest every year instead and earned 8%, after 30 years they would have an extra $181,700. With auto, college and even mortgage loans, the interest snowball is a little smaller because rates are lower, but you'd still much rather throw it than get hit by it.

Brad Reagan, "Live Debt-Free,"
Smart Money, *September 20, 2007.*

Track Your Cash

You should be able to identify your spending pattern in order to achieve financial success. Budgeting monthly and tracking your debts are ways to track your cash and expenses. This step is key to becoming debt free. Just ask the Weavers. They make note of what they spend and find ways of cutting costs wherever possible. Although they now live in a $275,000 home in the exclusive Southland subdivision and their neighbors are doctors, lawyers, and executives who drive shiny Mercedeses, Lexuses, and Jaguars, the Weavers live on a strict budget. Because they do, they can put all of their extra money into savings and investments. "We have always lived below our means and do not try to compete with others," states Triscilla. "We don't have the nicest car or biggest house because we focus on what is comfortable and meets the needs of our family."

Amazingly, the Weavers have been able to remain practically debt free even though Triscilla has been attending school over the past 13 years. Most people use student loans as an excuse for being in debt. But the Weavers consider the investment as another bill that requires planning. Since their marriage, Triscilla has worked full-time while pursuing her bachelor of science and master's degrees in middle-childhood education. She is now working on her doctorate, which she will complete in 2001.

"We've spent $45,000 of our own money already. I have never gotten a student loan. We set the criteria that I would only take classes that we would be able to pay for," says Triscilla. "We would save the money for three months prior to the semester. My education has been a part of our monthly budget for the past 13 years."

Plan for the Future

Before you can achieve financial success, you must have clearly defined goals. When individuals are in debt, they have no financial security, no savings, and usually do not invest in 401(k) plans. "Being in debt prevents a [financially secure] future. You are transferring your wealth to the creditor," says Hunt.

"Being debt free relieves stress, and that plays a major role in your lifestyle," says Tony. "Since we are debt free, it allows us to save a great deal and to invest in our 6-year-old son T.J.'s future and our retirement."

To show individuals how to stay out of debt, Ric Edelman, a financial planner and the chairman of Edelman Financial Services, teaches a seminar called "Square One" that shows consumers how to get out of debt. "The first thing we do is teach consumers to examine their spending habits. Too often people have no idea where their money goes," says Edelman, who is the author of *The Truth About Money*. "We then show them how to reduce unnecessary spending and how to anticipate future spending. This allows us to focus on income and existing savings, and allows us to set up a plan to eliminate the existing debt."

Don't Expect Instant Miracles

You did not get into debt overnight and will not get out overnight. In a telephone survey it conducted in 1999, Myvesta.org found that consumers have an average of three cards with $1,751 in total credit card debt. If they make the minimum payment on that debt, it will take 28.6 years to pay off and will cost $4,172 in interest (calculated on an interest rate of 17.99%). Merely one late fee of $29 will add an additional 21 months and $350 in interest to the debt.

"For people carrying a balance, if you have the cash, pay it off. If not, just try to become more aggressive in paying off your debt," says Kidwell. . . .

"We specialize in helping people who are really in debt," says Kidwell. "Every person in debt is suffering from some type of depression. Debt is one of the leading causes of divorce, lack of sleep, and poor work performance. It is truly one of the deep dark secrets that people have. It robs them of their self-worth and keeps them from achieving dreams."

Seek Professional Help

Find someone who is knowledgeable in financial matters and ask him or her to assist you in achieving the financial freedom they enjoy. You may not know the best way to pay off your

debt or lack the motivation to do so. That's where the professionals come in. Debt-counseling organizations such as Consumer Credit Counseling Services offer free services that include showing you how to create a budget, helping you to set
up a payment plan with creditors, and negotiating lower rates
on credit cards.

But before you contact anyone else, though, order your
credit report to see where you stand. The three main agencies
are Experian, Equifax, and TransUnion.

Books and newsletters are helpful as well. Hunt, who has
been publishing the monthly newsletter *Cheapskate Monthly*
for nine years, has seen people come out of debt only to go
right back in. She focuses on teaching people how to remain
debt free. "You should live in such a way that you are constantly prepared for the unexpected, like getting the car fixed
and buying a new refrigerator. To me, that is the essence of
debt-proof living."

Scarborough, who is married to Kenneth and has a 2-year-
old daughter named Desiree, is proud of her decision to
change her spending habits. "It was a joy to become debt free.
I invest in my 401(k), am working on putting money in my
savings, and have goals in terms of buying a home," she contends. "But I was also fearful at first because I wondered if I
could remain debt free for the rest of my life. It was kind of
like being an addict. That was 14 years of being in debt.
Through spiritual growth, I came to realize that we have a responsibility to ourselves and family members to be in positive
financial situations. Now, I am mindful and careful of everything I spend."

How Much Do I Owe?

In order to get out of debt, you need to know how much you
owe. Making a list will give you a clear picture of your personal financial situation, allowing you to begin the process of

managing your finances in a way that serves your needs. This is an important step to living debt free.

It's helpful to know the exact payoff dates of loans. However, it's more difficult to calculate the payoff date for credit card debts because minimum monthly payments go down as the amount of debt is reduced. In addition, interest varies because it's calculated based on the balance.

> "Generation Y watches as parents and neighbors lose their homes to foreclosure and their grandparents try to stretch Social Security to cover basic needs."

Living Debt-Free Is Not Always Possible

USA Today (Magazine)

USA Today (Magazine) *is a monthly periodical published by the Society for the Advancement of Education. The following article explains the vast amount of debt with which Generation Y must deal and the difficulty and unrealistic nature of living debt-free within the Y Generation.*

As you read, consider the following questions:

1. On average, how much is a student's loan bill?

2. What percentage of college graduates owe at least $5,000 on credit cards?

3. According to self-made millionaire James White, what is one reason Generation Y is in debt?

"Another Fine Mess for Generation Y (Student Loans)," USA Today (Magazine), December 2008.

Some 40% of recent college graduates have more than $10,000 in student loan debt and over 20% owe at least $5,000 on credit cards before age 25, according to a Harris Interactive study. "Generation Y is in some serious money trouble," says international empire-builder James White, a 23-year-old self-made millionaire, motivational speaker, and author of *My First Million*.

"My age group spends tens of thousands of dollars to go to college and then owes thousands of dollars more in student loans and credit cards before they get their first paycheck."

Living Debt-Free Is Not Realistic for the Younger Generation

Teenagers and young adults are growing up at a different time of history than their parents or grandparents. They are not part of "the greatest generation" of Depression-fueled frugal spenders. They are not coming-of-age in the baby boomer "me" generation of spendthrifts that uses credit to purchase everything and anything without considering the consequences. This group of young adults is witnessing the American economy bottom out in deep recession. Generation Y watches as parents and neighbors lose their homes to foreclosure and their grandparents try to stretch Social Security to cover basic needs. Still, this group of young adults juggles bills and hopes for a money miracle.

"We know we don't want to spend ourselves into disaster, but we also don't want to give up the finer things in life," explains White. "Completely saying 'no' to debt isn't realistic for my generation. The problem is young people don't know a thing about how to make money, let alone make their money work for them."

White suggests it is not too late to guide young men and women toward success with money. He believes basic finance should be taught in high school. "This is one of the few things

"So, this is debt-free living."

we can't rely on the parents to teach at home because many adults are just learning the consequences for bad spending habits themselves."

America's Financial Future Is in Trouble

Time is running out, though. With each passing year, Generation Y spends itself more deeply into debt. The average student loan bill is $19,000, according to Sen. Edward Kennedy's Ensuring Continued Access to Student Loans Act of 2008. Payments tend to span 15 years, ensuring most students will remain in debt into their mid-30s.

The U.S. needs a fast financial reality check, White asserts. "We are the next generation of leaders and taxpayers. If someone doesn't reach out and explain the disaster we are headed for, America's financial future will come crumbling down like a house of cards."

> "You contracted the debt, and the deal
> your creditor cuts to get that money
> shouldn't be your concern."

Debtors Should Be More Conscientious Toward Creditors

Michelle Singletary

In the following viewpoint, Michelle Singletary, a radio host for Washington Post Radio and NPR's Day to Day, *argues that consumers should pay back their debt. She asserts that borrowers are morally obligated to pay their creditors, and concerns about the exorbitant profits being made by debt collection agencies are unfounded. According to recent studies, debt collection companies barely collect the money actually owed. Singletary notes, it does not matter how much profit those agencies are making, consumers should pay their debt regardless of who is collecting.*

As you read, consider the following questions:

1. What are the two types of debt collectors?

Michelle Singletary, "The Debt Is Yours Alone," *The Washington Post*, August 20, 2006, p. F01. Copyright © 2006, The Washington Post. Reprinted with permission.

2. According to ACA International, the Association of Credit and Collection Professionals, what percentage of the original debt is considered a reasonable commission?

3. According to the ACA, what amount of the debt collected by agencies in 2005 was purchased debt?

Let me address the common misconception that all debt collectors own the debt they're trying to collect.

Before I do that, however, I'd like to start with how my recent columns on debt collection began. I received a letter from an entrepreneur who had fallen on hard times but had recovered financially. She wanted to know if she should pay an old credit card debt in full. She owed $24,000, but a collection agency was offering to settle it for $14,000. Something didn't sit right with her. She wanted to pay the entire debt to clear her conscience.

I said to go with her conscience. And she did. She paid the $24,000.

Many people wrote to me, stunned that I would recommend such a thing. They argued that the debt collector was a third party who bought the original debt as a business investment, and therefore the woman shouldn't feel obligated to repay the full amount.

"Unfortunately, her creditor didn't receive a penny of the settlement amount that [she] paid," wrote Jerry Harold of Leesburg. "The debt collector bought the debt and collection rights at risk with the hope of collecting more than the discounted purchase price. When [she] paid the full balance, every penny went to the credit collector."

Robert D. Brougham of Denver wrote, "The moral obligation of debt can certainly be a factor to the originator of the debt, but once that lender has decided to discount the debt for his own business reasons, your position simply results in a windfall for the discount purchaser."

In other words, these writers considered this woman a chump. I couldn't help but wonder why.

Of course, on reflection, I do know why. We've become a society so used to the system playing us that we feel justified in playing the system.

Your Obligation to Pay

We ask ourselves: Why play fair if corporate America doesn't? In the case of credit card debt in particular, we figure the companies are raking in huge profits by charging high interest rates so if some debtors default, the lenders are getting what they deserve. It becomes easy to argue that if a company bought our debt for pennies on the dollar, why should we pay more than that?

There are two reasons why it matters. First, you are morally obligated. You contracted the debt, and the deal your creditor cuts to get that money shouldn't be your concern.

Second, creditors are not playing as many games as you think.

There are two types of debt collectors, those who work on commission and get a percentage of the debt they collect, and those who purchase the debt at a discount. Debt purchasers contract to buy debt from companies, usually for pennies on the dollar. It is true that a creditor who sells a portfolio of past-due accounts relinquishes all rights, titles and interest to the accounts once the sale of the debt is closed. But again, that's between the creditor and the debt purchaser.

Nonetheless, the overwhelming majority of collection agencies are working on a commission and are collecting debt on behalf of the borrower's creditor.

Commission debt collectors do not own title to the debt. These agencies collect on delinquent accounts referred to them by various credit grantors, such as credit card issuers, banks, retail stores, hospitals and other health-care services, or by federal, state and local governments. It is true the agencies

The Debt Collection Industry Is Essential to the Economy

ACA International, the Association of Credit and Collection Professionals (ACA) today [June 28, 2006] released a new study that demonstrates, for the first time, the value of the third-party collection industry to the U.S. economy. The landmark study reveals that the industry returned $39 billion in 2005 to businesses that extend consumers credit.

The economic effect of this debt collection activity has been to keep prices lower, thus saving the average American household $351. The report, titled "Value of Third-Party Debt Collection to the U.S. Economy: Survey and Analysis," was authored by global advisory firm PricewaterhouseCoopers LLP and based on a national survey of third-party debt collection firms. . . .

The study reveals a growing, positive impact of employment in the third-party debt collection industry, which has more than doubled in the last 15 years—from fewer than 70,000 employees in 1990 to nearly 150,000 in 2005. The direct and indirect economic impact models used in the study estimate that the industry, including business purchases and personal purchases by its owners and workers, supported a total of 426,700 American jobs with payroll totaling $15 billion in 2005.

ACA International, the Association of Credit and Collection Professionals, National Study Finds Debt Collection Industry Essential to U.S. Economy, *June 28, 2006.*

charge a hefty fee for their services. Generally, 33 percent of the original debt is considered a reasonable commission, said Rozanne M. Andersen, general counsel and senior vice president of legal and government affairs for ACA International, the Association of Credit and Collection Professionals.

For the first time, in an effort to demonstrate the value of the collection industry, ACA surveyed collection agencies to find out just how much is being returned to creditors.

In the survey, conducted by PricewaterhouseCoopers LLP, ACA found that of the $141 billion in bad debt charged off by private businesses in 2005, third-party debt collection agencies recovered about $51.4 billion. Subtract the cut to the agencies, and $39.3 billion was returned to creditors.

Most of that was collected on commission. Of the debt collected by agencies in 2005, just $2.3 billion was on purchased debt, the ACA report found.

There are, without a doubt, a number of agencies that have given people reason to have disdain and distrust for the debt collection industry. Without question, the penalties, interest and fees on some debt can be monstrous and immoral. But this is more about our collective feelings about the companies charged with collecting debt. Let's say you're buying a home and you find out that the seller paid an incredibly low price for it. Would you argue that the homeowner shouldn't get the fair-market asking price because she paid so little for the home?

This same principle applies to legitimate and legal debt collection efforts. It is none of your business what a debt purchaser paid for your debt. And it certainly is none of your business what commission a debt collector is getting to collect on money you clearly and morally owe.

> *"From a moral standpoint the denunciation of interest charging is based on the principle that it is an imposition of the rich on the poor."*

Creditors Should Be More Conscientious Toward Debtors

Brian Alderson

In the following viewpoint, Brian Alderson, chairman of the Edgar Cayce Society of New Zealand, argues that charging debtors interest rates above and beyond inflation is immoral. Not only is it against Christian principles, but charging such high rates of interest acts as a form of slavery with affluent members of society exploiting the poor. As a result, the inflation rate grows and the economy is negatively affected.

As you read, consider the following questions:

1. What is the meaning of the Parable of the Talents?

2. What was the result of the Act of Henry VIII in England in 1545?

3. Which is the only major religion that continues to ban the practice of charging interest?

Brian Alderson, "The Sin of Interest," *The Best of The Rainbow Journal*, March 1, 2007. Reproduced by permission.

The rich ruleth over the poor, and the borrower is servant to the lender.—Proverbs 22:7

Historically the charging of interest on loans was considered, at the very least, immoral if not a transgression against the laws of God. This repugnance to interest stems from both the religious view that charging interest, especially exorbitant interest, was a sin, and the moral standpoint that interest was a flagrant expression of greed.

According to the Laws of Moses, the charging of interest on loans is a sin. Although like many statements in the Bible, if taken literally, the quotations can be interpreted in different ways (that is why there were so many lawyers!).

We read in Exodus 22:25 "If you lend money to my people, to the poorest among you—you shall not extract interest from them." But in Deuteronomy 23:20 "On loans to a foreigner you may charge interest, but on loans to another Israelite you may not charge interest."

There are other quotations, mostly in the Old Testament, that generally condemn interest and in the Sermon on the Mount Jesus emphasised that one should lend without concern for a return—or even repayment. However, those who support the principle of interest would be quick to quote the Parable of the Talents, which is the story of a servant who did not increase the money given to him by his master. "But his master replied, 'You wicked and lazy slave! You knew, did you, that I reap where I did not sow and gather where I did not scatter? Then you ought to have invested my money with the bankers, and on my return I would have what was my own with interest'" (Matthew 25:27).

Nevertheless in early times Christianity forbade interest charging in general, and in fact from 1179 those who practised it were excommunicated. Judaism followed the commandment not to charge interest to fellow Israelites. Later Islam, following the teachings of Mohammed, also forbade the imposition of interest. In the English speaking world a key

Payday Loan Facts and Stats

- Payday loans cost consumers over $4.2 billion in predatory fees each year.

- The typical payday borrower pays back $793 for a $325 loan.

- Ninety percent of the payday industry's revenues come from consumers who get five or more loans in a year.

- For two-week payday loans, finance charges result in interest rates from 390% to 780% APR [annual percentage rate]. The first APR is for a fee of $15 per $100 borrowed, the second APR results from a fee of $30 per $100 borrowed.

- The fifteen states (and DC) which have banned payday lending, are saving their residents a total of $1.8 billion per year in predatory payday loan fees.

- There are more payday stores in the United States than McDonald's restaurants. At the start of 2008, industry analysts claimed that about 23,600 payday storefronts were in operation.

Americans for Fairness in Lending,
"Facts and Stats," 2009. www.affil.org.

change was for the permission to charge interest by an Act of Henry VIII in England in 1545. Nowadays of the three religions it appears that only Islam continues to ban the practice.

Interest as a Moral Injustice

Since the time of Henry VIII the acceptance of interest charging has permeated throughout the Western world although up until recent times most Western governments imposed controls on credit and strict limits of the amount of interest that could be charged and usury, in the sense of exorbitantly high rates of interest, was often illegal. Nowadays, at a time of globalisation, deregulation, free trade and 'letting market forces prevail,' we see very little control and regulation of credit and interest. In fact a number of governments are in on the game by setting up schemes to loan money to young people for their education.

From a moral standpoint the denunciation of interest charging is based on the principle that it is an imposition of the rich on the poor. It is the rich who have the money available to lend and who extract interest from the poor whose only way of repaying the interest as well as the principal, is by working for the money which brings about a form of economic slavery.

It is considered morally unjust that by merely having money the moneyed people can live and prosper without having to work and still retain the money they have. As an example: Bill has an inheritance of $1 million and lends the money at 6% interest to Fred. Bill now receives $60,000 a year so does not need to work for a living and at the same time he retains ownership of the $1 million. What is happening here is that Fred is now working as an economic slave to Bill to the amount of $60,000 a year until the loan is repaid. The amount of time Fred must spend in this slavery will depend on Fred's capacity to earn money. In reality Bill will probably place the money in an interest bearing account with a bank or other lending institution in which case 'Fred' may be a number of borrowers who each would be mortgaged for some time working to pay Bill his interest.

Another reason given for denouncing interest is that the poorer one becomes the greater the amount of interest one is charged.

Inflated Interest

One may argue that lenders must be able to cover inflation and risks which can eat away at one's capital and would therefore justify interest. If the interest was only used to cover this inflation then there would be little cause for concern. I recently witnessed a loan from one of our 'money shops' in which the interest rate was 29.95% per annum [year] on top of various administration charges which, if included with the actual interest charged, would amount to the equivalent of 69% per annum interest! These rates are by no means uncommon and these lending institutions charging these rates target the poorest section of our community.

What is becoming of great concern these days is that ethics seem to be disappearing from much of our business world where greed is no longer considered a vice but a virtue. If Scrooge were conducting his business today it would be under the banner of 'Scrooge Limited' and as a company would receive accolades for business excellence. Banks in particular, the backbone of our finance industry used to be looked up to for their integrity and business ethics, however, we now observe the major banks being involved in shady deals and illegal overcharging in the frantic efforts to satisfy their shareholders' insatiable appetites for profits.

It is interesting to note that while in general Western governments have taken an attitude of 'laissez faire' [hands off] to commerce in general, when it comes to controlling inflation, the governments are very much involved. Inflation in the main has the least effect on the lower income working class, particularly where wages tend to rise in line with prices. Those most affected are the rich, particularly those with large cash assets and money invested in loans. As our opening quote from Proverbs states, 'The rich ruleth over the poor,' so it is these people who have ensured that governments do everything possible to curb inflation and thus preserve the wealth of the affluent. Yet it is this very matter of charging interest

charged by those affluent people that puts a constant infla-
tionary pressure on the value of money.

While the above comments only briefly touch on a subject
of interest, which can be quite a complex issue, I trust the
foregoing will leave you with food for thought. Our current
economic system has a number of intrinsic flaws, and the
negative results of our present policies on interest need to be
addressed if we are to curb the widening gap between the
haves and have-nots and the inability of the wealthy countries
to address the basic needs of much of the world's population.

Periodical Bibliography

The following articles have been selected to supplement the diverse views presented in this chapter.

Oren Bar-Gill and Kevin Davis	"Flexible, Responsible Credit-Card Reform," *Business Week Online*, May 7, 2009.
Justin Fox	"The Paradox of Thrift," *Time*, February 23, 2009.
Carla Fried	"The Rate Is Worth the Pain," *Money*, May 2009.
Thomas Geoghegan	"Infinite Debt," *Harper's Magazine*, April 2009.
Daniel Gross	"Debt Be Not Proud," *Newsweek*, April 20, 2009.
Dan Kadlec	"How the Crisis Is Changing You," *Money*, May 2009.
Zachary Karabell	"The Biggest Thing to Fear Is Fear," *Newsweek*, March 16, 2009.
Jill Lepore	"I.O.U.," *The New Yorker*, April 13, 2009.
William J. Lynott	"The New Rules for Personal Finances," *Ophthalmology Times*, April 15, 2009.
John Maggs	"Fiscal Responsibility Starts Early," *National Journal*, May 19, 2009.
Gene Marks	"When Tight Credit Is the Right Credit," *Business Week Online*, May 4, 2009.
Jeffrey D. Sachs	"Rethinking the Global Money Supply," *Scientific American*, June 2009.
Mark Steyn	"Closing Up Shop," *National Review*, April 20, 2009.
Rob Walker	"Brother, Can You Spare a Loan?" *The New York Times Magazine*, May 17, 2009.

CHAPTER 2

Do Some People Struggle to Manage Debt Responsibly?

Chapter Preface

Payday loans, or cash advances loaned against a future paycheck, are not new, but lately they have caused controversy as the need for them has increased due to the state of the national economic situation. The procedure for taking out a payday loan is simple: a lender will loan a customer a certain portion of their next paycheck for a fee. Typically, the fee is $15 for every $100 borrowed, which means that if a person borrows $200 from their next paycheck, then they will repay the lender $230. Often people turn to payday lenders to help them when they are faced with an emergency requiring immediate cash, but not everyone is supportive of the payday loan industry. In fact, some states such as New York have banned payday loans altogether, stating that they exploit the poor.

Industry leaders and the customers they serve stand behind payday loans, saying that they provide an important service to the community. In an opinion piece in *The Roanoke Times* on July 29, 2007, Kevin Doyle, a Virginia-based regional manager for payday lender Quik Cash, says, "The payday advance industry exists because it fills a vacuum that banks created when they stopped offering low-dollar, short-term loans." His views are echoed by other supporters, who argue that payday loans are a good alternative to banks and other lenders that require a credit check for cash-strapped customers with a history of bad credit. In an editorial in *USA Today* on October 2, 2006, Darrin Andersen, president of the Community Financial Services Association of America, echoes Doyle's statement, "Customers choose payday advances because it costs less than bouncing a check or paying overdraft fees, late bill penalties or credit card late fees, and it is more desirable than asking family for money or pledging personal possessions."

For opponents of payday loans, the practice is not as noble. In recent years many consumer advocates and lawmakers have charged payday loan companies with usury, the practice of charging exorbitant interest rates. According to a 2009 study by the Center for Responsible Lending, "Payday loans carry annual interest rates of 400 percent and are designed to catch working people—or those with a steady source of income such as Social Security or a disability check—in a long-term debt trap." In other words, customers borrow money against their paychecks, but then have difficulty paying the money back and paying their other bills, so they continue to borrow more money until they are unable to pay back the original loan amount. In order to stop this vicious cycle, what some critics have referred to as predatory lending, consumer watchdogs have turned to the federal government to pass laws limiting the amount of interest and the number of loan renewals that payday loan companies can charge. To that end, Congress passed a law in 2007 limiting the interest on payday loans to military personnel to 36 percent. Supporters are pushing for that rate to apply to all customers.

One of the biggest claims made against payday loan companies is that they abuse minorities and the poor. Supporters argue that these groups need to manage their finances better. The authors in this chapter debate whether some groups of people manage their credit more effectively than others. Some argue it should be up to individuals to decide if they want to take the risk of borrowing against their paychecks.

| "Ideally, discussing how people use and abuse money starts early and continues well after boxes are packed for college."

Young People Should Have Credit Cards

Jonathan Burton

Jonathan Burton is assistant personal finance editor at Market-Watch.com. In the following viewpoint, he argues that teenagers can learn money management strategies by being given credit cards. This can help them understand how money works and how to budget their finances to get the items they want. He also encourages parents to talk to their children about money and to show them how to balance a checkbook. By giving young people these skills while there is relatively little risk to their economic well-being, parents can prepare their children for healthy financial futures.

As you read, consider the following questions:

1. Why are the teenage years a good time to introduce young people to money management strategies?

2. According to a Schwab survey, what percentage of respondents knew how to use credit cards?

3. According to Carrie Schwab Pomerantz, what percentage of bankruptcies are from people age 35 or younger?

For many parents, talking about money with their teenagers begins and ends with "How much do you need?" Of course, the financial facts of life are more complicated and, like that other Big Talk, the sooner you and your kids have it, the better. "This is a critical life skill," says Carrie Schwab Pomerantz, chief strategist of consumer education at Charles Schwab & Co., Inc. "Kids want to learn, and they would like to learn from their parents and have them as role models."

Most parents want their children to know what it means to earn, save, spend and share money. But starting that conversation can be awkward. Schools don't offer much in the way of financial planning, while many adults face emotional obstacles where money equates to love, or control or self-image. Maybe families aren't managing their own finances, or it could be that the subject of money is simply taboo.

"We live in such an affluent society today that it's even more important to teach kids responsibility for themselves and for others," says Pomerantz, who notes that having brokerage founder Charles Schwab as a father didn't give her any advantage about finances.

"My father wasn't necessarily one to have money conversations," she says. "I did not get an allowance, I've had jobs since I was 13 years old."

Ideally, discussing how people use and abuse money starts early and continues well after boxes are packed for college. If that hasn't happened yet in your family, the teen years are especially crucial: Kids of that age are keen to have cash and will find many innovative uses for it. For everything else, there's the credit card. So it's a good time for kids to learn about budgeting and bill paying, saving and spending.

Budgeting and Spending

What teens don't know about money was evident in a recent Schwab survey. Only 45% of respondents knew how to use credit cards, while just 26% understood credit card interest and fees. About 40% said they could budget themselves, but only one in three could read a bank statement, balance a checkbook and pay bills. And barely one in five had any inkling about how to invest.

Ross Levin, a financial adviser in Edina, Minn., teaches his teenage daughters about budgeting by giving them a set amount of money each month for clothes, entertainment and other personal expenses. If the girls are with their parents and want to buy something but don't have the money, Levin says there's no prearranged deal allowing them to pay it back.

"They have their money, they bring their money, they spend their money," Levin says, adding that the strict policy has been a lesson for the entire family.

"It's a very different feeling when you're making the decision and doling out the dollars," he says. "We found them making choices they didn't make when we were the ATM."

Credit Cards

Budgeting is all about choices and limits. Credit cards break through the budget wall. "Charge it" is liberating, gratifying, and easy to say and do. But credit card debt can also break a bank account. That plastic card is real money, and monthly interest and related charges add up quickly.

"Credit card debt is insidious," says Pomerantz. "Thirty-five percent of bankruptcies are from young people 35 and under. We need to teach our kids to pay cash as much as possible and to use credit cards for emergencies. Do not put more on your credit card than you can pay off that month."

So although it seemingly violates parenting's cardinal rule about kids not playing with matches, some financial experts advocate giving teens a credit card.

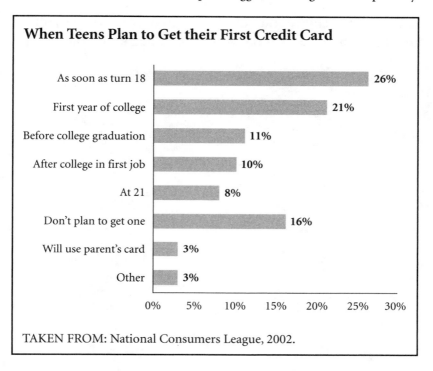

When Teens Plan to Get their First Credit Card

As soon as turn 18	26%
First year of college	21%
Before college graduation	11%
After college in first job	10%
At 21	8%
Don't plan to get one	16%
Will use parent's card	3%
Other	3%

TAKEN FROM: National Consumers League, 2002.

Says Pomerantz: "They need to know how to use a credit card, how interest accumulates, how fees are charged. They need to understand how to manage their credit."

Think of a credit card as a driver's license, and money as the family car. In novice hands both cars and credit cards can be dangerous. But a responsible young person who can practice and build skills under parental supervision is better prepared for the road.

Balancing and Bill Paying

Balancing a checkbook every month isn't high on most people's list of fun things to do. Yet squaring a bank statement with your own records is a basic tenet of financial management—and if your kids are looking over your shoulder, they might even catch a misplaced decimal point or two.

"I see mistakes all the time on bank statements," says Barbara Steinmetz, a financial adviser in Burlingame, Calif. "Take control of it. The checkbook is something you balance, and a credit card bill is something you read, to make sure the charges are all yours."

> "With so many expenses, today's youth are catching up with their parents, charging about $158 billion annually."

Young People Should Not Have Credit Cards

Carolyn M. Brown

Carolyn M. Brown is a contributor to Black Enterprise, *a magazine that provides business news and is an investment resource for African Americans. In the following viewpoint, Brown tells the story of Evelyn Sterling and the debt Evelyn has incurred since she received her first credit card at the age of 19. With the expenses of teens increasing, they are being lured by credit card companies into applying for credit, thus incurring debt at a young age.*

As you read, consider the following questions:

1. According to the article, what is the quickest way to poor credit?

2. How long are charge-offs, bad debts, and late payments included in an individual's credit history?

3. According to the viewpoint, for what major purchases will you want to have clean credit?

Carolyn M. Brown, "Beware of Credit Card Offers ($s and sense)," *Black Enterprise*, October 2002.

Evelyn Sterling was 19 when she got her first credit card—a MasterCard with a $500 limit. "At the time it seemed like easy money. I figured I can buy something now and just pay back the money later," says Evelyn, who was attending a local college in Chicago at the time and didn't have a full-time job. Looking to increase her balance, she applied for a second MasterCard six months later. This time her limit was $1,500.

By the time she turned 25, Evelyn had six credit cards (including store charge cards) and more than $5,500 in debt. She started falling behind on her payments and one of her creditors, Spiegel, canceled her card. She still owes $1,300 on that account. Evelyn, who is now 26 and working as a ministry director at Salem Baptist Church in Chicago, spent the past year reducing her debt. The first step was canceling all but one of her credit cards. She also took 13 weeks of debt management classes at her church.

Luring Teens into Debt

Yet, Evelyn is no different than many young people who build up debt before they have adequate means to pay it off. But what teen doesn't like to shop at the mall or online, which typically requires you to use a credit card? Like their peers, teenagers spend money on clothes, CDs, books, food, and gas.

With so many expenses, today's youth are catching up with their parents, charging about $158 billion annually. Some Congressional leaders have sought to restrict credit cards use among people under the age of 21, arguing that credit card issuers lure unsuspecting teens into debt. They also want to end credit card soliciting on college campuses.

Building Credit

Getting a charge card can be a way to build a good credit record, which is invaluable when you are ready to get a car, mortgage, or even a small business loan, says Pierre Dunagan, financial advisor and principal of the Dunagan Group in Chi-

Prepaid Credit Cards for Teens

The prepaid credit card works much the same way as a gift card. The parent will load money onto the card, which then can be used at any retail or merchant that accepts the credit card company that issued the prepaid card. There are several benefits to using such a card including:

- Convenience
- Security
- A lesson in budgeting
- Parents can track spending habits
- The cards have overdraft protection
- A limit is placed on spending
- No overdraft fees
- No interest charges

Joseph Kenny,
"Prepaid Credit Cards: A Suitable Substitution for Teens,"
October 17, 2008. www.jsnet.org.

cago. "It is also good to have in case of an emergency." Instead of calling a parent to wire money, a college student could use his or her card, for instance.

However, nothing can lead to poor credit quicker than the misuse of credit cards—several cards in one's name, huge unpaid balances, and late payments. Keep in mind that bad debts don't disappear from your credit once they have been paid. Your credit history includes charge-offs, bad debts, and late payments for a period of seven years.

If you have plans to buy a car, a house, or any other major purchase, you will want to have a clean credit report and a low credit score. Your credit report is a summary of your past and present accounts, including credit cards. And your credit, or FICO, score is a number based on all late payments and outstanding debts. This number ranges from about 400 to 800.

> *"Blacks and whites appear to have dif-*
> *ferent spending habits only because*
> *blacks tend to be concentrated in poor*
> *communities more than whites."*

Class, as Well as Race, Contributes to Frivolous Spending

Wharton School of the University of Pennsylvania

The Wharton School of the University of Pennsylvania is a busi-
ness program dedicated to educating others about personal and
corporate finance. In the following viewpoint, they discuss the
findings of a recent study conducted by Nikolai Roussanov and
others, which challenges the belief that African Americans spend
their money frivolously. They found that social class was an even
better indicator of whether consumers buy clothes, jewelry, and
other nonessential items because expensive, visible purchases al-
low even the poorest people to create the appearance of wealth.

As you read, consider the following questions:

1. How much more do blacks and Hispanics spend on visible items than whites of comparable income?

Wharton School of the University of Pennsylvania, "Conspicuous Consumption and
Race: Who Spends More on What," Knowledge@Wharton, May 14, 2008. Copyright ©
2008 The Wharton School of the University of Pennsylvania. Reproduced by permission.

2. About how much less do blacks and Hispanics than whites of similar income spend on education?

3. Which group of Americans, regardless of social class, do not spend money on visible goods?

Fashionable clothes, jewelry, flashy cars . . . They are all items of conspicuous consumption that give their owners status on the street.

Some groups, such as blacks and Hispanics, seem to spend more on such emblems of success than others. Or is that just a stereotype?

Comedian Bill Cosby has long condemned his own black community for spending too much on flashy goods at the expense of children's education. He has been roundly criticized by some and praised by others, but there hasn't been much evidence to show whether his claims are true. Those who believe spending patterns vary among racial and ethnic groups typically invoke cultural differences, but there hasn't been much solid evidence of that, either.

"Blacks do spend more on these things—jewelry, clothing and cars—that have something to do with visibility," says Wharton finance professor Nikolai Roussanov. "Is it just taste? Or does it have to do with a social status component?"

Keeping Up with the Joneses

Economists have long accepted the explanation for conspicuous consumption presented by Norwegian-American economist Thorstein Veblen, who coined the term at the end of the 19th century. Valuable possessions visible to all are a signal of one's wealth, success and status, Veblen said. Today, most people recognize that spending decisions are influenced by the desire to "keep up with the Joneses."

In looking deeper at the subject, Roussanov and his collaborators, Kerwin Kofi Charles and Erik Hurst of the University of Chicago, found some truth to the ethnic stereotypes on spending, but they concluded that the explanation lies in economics, not culture. Their work is described in a paper titled, "Conspicuous Consumption and Race."

"If you're a middle-class black, it seems like in order to be perceived by whites and other blacks as relatively well off, you have to show you have money," Roussanov says. "You have to spend more on things that are observable."

To examine spending by racial groups, Roussanov and his colleagues studied data collected from 1986 to 2002 for the Consumer Expenditure Survey conducted by the federal Bureau of Labor Statistics. Blacks and Hispanics spend up to 30% more than whites of comparable income on visible goods like clothing, cars and jewelry, the researchers found. This meant that compared to white households of similar income, the typical black and Hispanic household spent $2,300 more per year on visible items. To do that, they spent less on almost all other categories except housing, and they saved less.

Visible items are those others can see when one is in public. The researchers found that blacks and Hispanics do not spend more than whites on items, such as home furnishings, that could serve as status symbols but aren't seen by as many people.

Alabama vs. Massachusetts

While Roussanov and his colleagues acknowledge that cultural preferences may play a role in these spending choices, they tested that theory by subdividing blacks, Hispanics and whites by income level and state of residence. This caused the differences in spending patterns to disappear. What really matters, Roussanov, Charles and Hurst found, is not one's race but one's economic situation relative to the "reference group"— people in the immediate community. "This is not really about race in the end. It is simply about what we observe about you and what peer group you belong to," Roussanov says.

Poor blacks and poor whites both spend more on visible goods if they live in poor communities, because such spending gives them more status relative to others in the community. But poor blacks and poor whites living among wealthier people do not devote extra portions of income to visible expenditures, since they are too far behind to get more status from the extra spending they can afford. Moreover, the very fact of belonging to a particular group provides observers with information about one's likely income (e.g., blacks are on average poorer than whites).

A low income white person in Alabama, for example, is likely to spend more on visible goods than a low income white person in Massachusetts. That's because white people are generally poorer in Alabama; in wealthy Massachusetts, spending more on visible goods is a waste of money, since it does not boost one's status.

Blacks and whites appear to have different spending habits only because blacks tend to be concentrated in poor communities more than whites, Roussanov says. Nationally, the poor white is likely to be surrounded by many whites who are not as poor, so he or she cannot afford to use conspicuous consumption to compete for status. But a black person of the same income is more likely to be surrounded by others of similar income, making this competition feasible.

In all races, people of a given income become less and less likely to emphasize conspicuous consumption as they get farther and farther behind their neighbors financially. "The overall predominance of conspicuous consumption between blacks and whites is really not a black-white phenomenon; it is simply an artifact of the environment," Roussanov says. "Blacks are poorer in this country, and so are Hispanics."

The research suggests that Cosby and others are wrong to blame cultural reasons for spending priorities—or are oversimplifying the matter. But that does not mean these critics are wrong about the consequences. Money spent on conspicu-

The Culture of Bling

Donald Trump's latest "Apprentice," Dr. Randal D. Pinkett, went "Old School" on young African Americans yesterday [in 2006] in an appearance at The College of New Jersey [TCNJ], ripping what he called their glitzy lifestyle of "nothingness."

"We're becoming far too materialistic," Pinkett said before a predominantly African American audience. "We place more value on how we look than what we know. Image is everything . . . we don't recognize that knowledge is the true sign of success."

Speaking at a Metropolitan Trenton African American Chamber of Commerce (MTAACC) gathering at the TCNJ Student Center celebrating Trenton Community Enrichment Day, Pinkett bared his heart and soul to the mostly black audience.

He belittled "these trendy clothes and cell phones and diamond necklaces and gold chains." . . .

"We have gone from Generation X to Generation Y to Generation B, and the B stands for bling-bling, and it don't mean a thing-thing!"

Jack Knarr,
"Donald Disciple Disses Decadence,"
Trentonian.com, January 29, 2006.

ous consumption must be diverted from other uses, and many studies have shown that blacks and Hispanics save less toward goals like college expenses and retirement than whites with the same income.

Roussanov and his colleagues find that blacks and Hispanics spend 16% and 30% less, respectively, on education than whites of similar income. They spend 50% less on health care.

Spending on health and education is not as visible to as many people as spending on cars and clothes, so it does not contribute as much to one's status.

Status vs. Fashion

The research indicates that spending habits are heavily influenced by a deep-seated yearning for status rather than transient fashion following. That could make the behavior harder to change, assuming that education, health and savings should come before shoes and jewelry.

Roussanov notes that spending on conspicuous consumption is not entirely counterproductive. In many communities, he says, it may be necessary to present a more affluent image to compete for jobs and to have a social life.

This may explain the chief exception the researchers found in the data: Older people don't spend more on visible goods, even if their incomes are the same as those of younger people who do. Perhaps it's the wisdom of age, or the fact that older people grew up in different times. But it's more likely, says Roussanov, that older people, regardless of their community, don't need status symbols as much because they're not out hunting for jobs and mates.

That reinforces the conclusion that spending for status is a deeply entrenched habit among those who do it. "It seems like health and education should receive more funding by individuals, but we can't simply force that on people and think it will make them better off," Roussanov says. "How do we promote going to an expensive college rather than buying an expensive watch? There's no simple fix to it."

The research, he notes, may have some practical implications for government policy and marketing.

This spring [2008], for example, millions of American households are receiving government checks as part of the economic stimulus package approved earlier in the year. Policy makers' predictions about how people will spend the money may turn out to be far off the mark, given what this research shows about spending incentives among different income groups, Roussanov suggests. "We cannot just assume that the same money is going to be spent the same way by people in different groups."

Marketers advertising cars, clothes and jewelry have long known of the higher demand for flashier products in poorer communities, Roussanov says. But the new insights might be useful, he notes, to companies marketing mutual funds or other financial services products that have yet to catch on in minority communities. The fact that saving and stock market participation is lower among minorities could be potentially linked to their greater spending on cars and other visible items.

A mutual fund investment is not the kind of possession that can be displayed on the street, making sales difficult for a company trying to sell funds to people who prize visible emblems of prosperity but are less tempted by the financial rewards far in the future. Perhaps one (although costly) way to overcome this problem, according to Roussanov, would be to set up branch offices in poorer communities. One could then gain status by being seen visiting a financial advisor. "If you want to make [investing] behavior more prominent," he says, "you have to make the behavior more visible."

> *"The real roots of the crisis ... have much to do with being forced to supplement stagnant real wages with expensive debt in order to keep up with climbing costs of living."*

Racism Is Responsible for the Minority Debt Crisis, Not Excessive Spending

David Crockett

David Crockett is a marketing professor at the University of South Carolina. His research focuses on the sociological aspect of consumer behavior and how racial inequality impacts the marketplace. In the following viewpoint, he argues that it is not the spending habits of African Americans that have caused the current credit crisis among black Americans. Instead, low wages, racism in the workplace, and exorbitant debt fees continue to support the myth of the foolish, overextended African American consumer. Until that myth is torn down, black families will remain in a financial stranglehold.

David Crockett, "Credit, Conspicuous Consumption and Crisis," *Black Commentator*, no. 132, March 31, 2005. Reproduced by permission of the author.

As you read, consider the following questions:

1. According to Demos, how do white and black families compare in terms of credit debt?

2. According to historian Ted Ownby, what are the origins of the myth of the frivolous black consumer?

3. How do some consumer behaviorists characterize black youth?

It seems that were it not for bad news there would be almost no news in Black America these days. Black folk, in case you hadn't heard, are in the midst of yet another crisis. This time it's a debt crisis, particularly in short-term revolving debt (primarily credit cards, but also payday loans, car title loans, etc.). Though Black families are less likely to have credit cards than White families those who do are much more likely to carry a monthly balance. According to data compiled by Demos from the most recent Survey of Consumer Finances (2001) just over half of White credit card holding families carry a monthly balance (averaging $4,381) while 84% of Black families carry monthly balances (averaging $2,950). Even though Black families carry smaller monthly balances a higher percentage of their financial worth goes into servicing debt. In addition, credit card balances alone do not fully reflect the total cost of debt paid by Black and Brown families, who are most likely to resort to the sub-prime underworld of pawn shops, check cashing joints, and car title lenders charging loan shark interest rates.

But wait, it gets worse. The bankruptcy bill,[1] which may have been signed, sealed and delivered by the time you read this, practically slams shut the one door available to consumers who are eventually overwhelmed by debt—personal bank-

---

1. The Bankruptcy Abuse Prevention and Consumer Protection Act of 2005 makes it more difficult for some consumers to file bankruptcy.

ruptcy. Though personal bankruptcies are often gut-wrenching economic and emotional affairs they do represent a way out of insurmountable debt.

Conspicuously Consuming Our Way to the Poorhouse?

Could the roots of fiscal crisis in Black America really lie in their conspicuous consumption as Bill Cosby has suggested? Are Black people conspicuously consuming their way into back-breaking debt, overly enamored of expensive athletic shoes instead of Hooked on Phonics? If so, what are we to make of folk who are living the life but living it largely on credit, well beyond their meager economic means?

I'll resist the urge to throw a mountain of data at you to debunk this powerful racial myth about Black consumption, but let's get something out of the way early. There is simply nothing in existing data to suggest that Black people's consumption is any more conspicuous, foolish, or short-sighted than anyone else's. Even in the categories where Blacks outspend Whites in many instances they are simply paying more than Whites for the same goods and services rather than consuming more (transportation and food are primary examples). Yet this powerful and enduring myth about conspicuous consumption, epitomized by Coz's "$500 sneakers," is repeated incessantly and seems to be remarkably resistant to contradictory data. I suppose this should not be especially surprising since powerful myths such as this are meant to transmit deeply held values by embedding them in images and stories. But understand this: The most important question to consider when debunking racial mythology is not whether it is true. If a myth is to stand the test of time it has to contain at least *some* truth, but just throwing inconsistent facts at it doesn't make it go away, either. The most important questions to ask in order to debunk powerful racial myths are what values do they transmit and whose interests do they serve?

Bound up in the all-too-easy-to-assimilate images and stories about the frivolous Black consumer is White supremacy, American racial mythology's most deeply held value. Though the oft-repeated stories about Black people's inherent foolishness pre-date the end of legal slavery these stories actually grew in importance afterward. After the Civil War the central debate in American social life was about how the newly freed slaves would participate in labor and consumer markets as well as in the polity. Historian Ted Ownby, in his outstanding *American Dreams in Mississippi*, notes that the stereotypical Black consumer mythologized during this period was indulgent, impulsive, and wasteful; the proverbial fool to be soon parted from his money. This myth has an enduring legacy in American history because it specified what could be expected from Blacks if they were allowed to participate fully in the marketplace. That is, the myth helped confirm that Black people's purchases would reflect their inherent character—indulgent, impulsive, wasteful, and self-destructive. Not coincidentally, it also confirmed that Whites' purchases would reflect their inherent character—responsible, independent, and free from vice.

This myth took root in the American sensibility long before anyone had data that could confirm it or disconfirm it. Once ground into the historical development of American consumer markets it became largely unfazed by counterfactual data. Its primary function was to justify anti-Black discrimination in the marketplace, thereby making Black people's presumed inferior status a self-fulfilling prophesy. Ownby notes the rhetorical catch-22 this mythology has presented for Blacks since slavery's end, especially for the working class and marginally poor. When Black people who live on the economic margins look the part, it affirms the notion that Black people lack the industry to attain material success. Yet when Black people, particularly working class Blacks, display the audacity to construct consumption-centered lifestyles it affirms their presumed inability to delay gratification.

The Frivolous Black Consumer Myth

So whose interests are served by the myth of the frivolous Black consumer? In one respect this is an easy question to answer. This mythology, and the dilemma it produces for Blacks, has consistently reinforced White supremacy, providing Whites with privileged status in the market in ways that are difficult to fully measure. Black consumption serves as a rhetorical counterpoint with which White consumption can be contrasted. It is worth noting that versions of this myth also portray other people of color and White women similarly, as irrational, impulsive, and wasteful. So this kind of mythologizing is hardly limited to Blacks. Still, in the United States the power of mythology to simply overwhelm reason reaches its apex when Black people are involved, even if only indirectly.

Consider for example the recent bankruptcy bill, a truly abhorrent piece of legislation, as a testament to how racial mythology helped set the boundaries of a debate without ever explicitly mentioning Black people. Chuck Grassley (R-IA), sponsor of the Senate version, quickly adopted the language of "irresponsible consumers" bailing out of their debts by declaring bankruptcy. Grassley dug directly into Ronald Reagan's time-tested trick bag of racialized code words and pulled out a bulletproof way to frame public discussion. Grassley's rhetoric made the bill practically immune to substantial counterevidence that consumer bankruptcies occur primarily after unfortunate or traumatic life events (like health crises) rather than too many trips to the mall. Couple this with the fact that the almost completely de-regulated, hugely profitable credit card industry is hardly in need of government protection from their most profitable consumers, those teetering on the edge of bankruptcy. It is of course beyond question that the credit card companies and the large sums of money they spend on The Hill [Capitol Hill] shepherded this bill through the process. But, lest you doubt the power of racial mythology to structure the terms of debate note that even politicians who opposed the bill did not directly challenge the "lifestyles of the greedy and frivolous" imagery championed by Grassley despite being provided with more than enough data by consumer advocates, bankruptcy lawyers, judges, and scholars to do so. Rather they couched their primary opposition in terms of the bill's impact on the "deserving poor" (e.g., seniors, children, those in ill health, and veterans). Well, you know who the greedy and frivolous are in the popular imagination don't you? If you don't, just ask your Uncle Charles (Barkley). He'll tell you at halftime of the next NBA game on TNT.

White supremacy isn't the only interest being served.

It would be foolish to suggest that White supremacy is the only value being transmitted through the frivolous Black consumption myth, though it is the most powerful. Still, stories about working class and poor Blacks who "love to look the part without keeping it real" are frequently part of a larger critique of the degraded state of Black America. This critique of current conditions commonly proffered by the Black middle classes highlights the dysfunctional behavior among the Black working class and poor as a key cause of community decline. For instance, in my recent research on the role of political ideology in consumer behavior my informants (from a Midwestern city) are highly critical of the Black working class, particularly Black youth. They critique Black youth consumption as overly frivolous (just like Coz, they went right to the sneakers) and prone to vices like stealing, vandalism, violence, etc. They cite this behavior as a key cause—if not the sole cause—of retail flight from predominantly Black areas of the city.

I do not dismiss whatever merit there may be to such claims. The deeper purpose served by this story, which people told me time and time again, however, was that it rendered their personal consumption choices less problematic by com-

The Black-White Spending Gap

In his controversial speech, Bill Cosby appealed to the African American community to start investing in their futures. What's troubling about the message of this study is that Cosby and others may not be battling against a black culture of consumption, but a more deeply seated human pursuit of status. In this sense, Cosby's critics may be right—only when black incomes catch up to white incomes will the apparent black-white gap in spending on visible goods disappear.

Ray Fisman, "Cos and Effect,"
Slate.com, January 11, 2008.

parison. That is, Black folk fortunate enough to attain middle class status are immediately faced with vexing questions about their consumption and its impact on those less-fortunate in the Black community. Move the family into a better school district in the suburbs or stay in the city? Continue to shop at Black neighborhood stores or patronize suburban stores that have better selection and lower prices? These questions do not have simple, pat answers. Highlighting the dysfunctional choices of others aids many in the middle class to frame their own choices, whatever they may be, as not only rational by comparison but as truly in the best interests of the Black community.

What Is to Be Done?

It is long past time we let go the myth that conspicuous consumption is destroying Black America's economy. Far too many Black people who get up and go to work every day continue to see shrinking wages, mounting credit card bills and slipping credit ratings for us to have so much invested in a fallacy. Far too much time has been spent running in fear from the image of the frivolous Black consumer. Far too much has been tolerated from those, Black and White, who have wielded the image as a weapon to mollify Black people's legitimate concerns about the sad economic state of affairs in Black America. Far too much attention has been diverted from the real roots of the current crisis.

The roots of the crisis have nothing to do with frivolous consumption. They have everything to do with welfare-level wages, an enormous racial wealth gap, and super-expensive debt. The real roots of the crisis for most people have much to do with being forced to supplement stagnant real wages with expensive debt in order to keep up with climbing costs of living. Black people and people generally in the U.S. are not so much spending way beyond their means as much as they are trying to carve out a meaningful life within them, and having to take on a ton of debt to do so. I wish I could offer some easy answers for a way out of this dilemma but if there were any we would have already found them. I can say with a fair degree of certainty that the only way out of this mess is through organizing for collective action.

Without taking up the specific merits of reparations [for slavery] in this article, if the way out of crisis is through organizing, I believe there is much to be learned from the ongoing struggle for reparations. With all due respect to the good people at *Black Enterprise*, I do not believe that chasing after personal financial empowerment in capital markets is an adequate response to Black America's fiscal crisis. Though I have nothing against Black people building personal wealth, as long as it is kept in perspective, such pursuits have no inherent political character. The economic crisis in Black America is inherently political. As such, the mere building of assets among a few individuals is not a sufficient response. Though reparations as a topic has moved from the margins to the center of debate in Black America as a social movement, it remains in its infancy. Still, I concur with Sundiata Cha-Jua's [director of African American Studies at University of Illinois at Urbana-Champaign] contention that we look to the reparations struggle as a model—if not a vehicle—for revitalizing Black civil society by coordinating social, political, and economic capital and by focusing on institution building in a participatory democratic culture. Whether it is reparations or some other issue, we have little choice but to organize and rebuild.

| "The facts belie the myth that women are filing [for bankruptcy] because they are irresponsible and frivolous spenders."

Women Are More Likely to Struggle with Finances than Men

Sandra Guy

In the following viewpoint, Sandra Guy, a business reporter for the Chicago Sun-Times, *argues that women are far more likely to file for bankruptcy than men because they tend to make lower wages, often have less education, and generally have sole responsibility for raising their children. Given these constraints, women are frequently forced into bankruptcy to remain financially stable. The bankruptcy law passed in 2005 limits consumers' abilities to file for bankruptcy, which could cripple women economically for many years to come.*

As you read, consider the following questions:

1. How many women filed for bankruptcy in 2005?

Sandra Guy, "Bankruptcy Law Pushes Women Closer to Edge," *Women's E-News*, October 27, 2005. Copyright © 2005 Women's eNews. Reproduced by permission. www.womensenews.org.

2. According to a nationwide survey, what percentage of women had less than $500 in emergency savings?

3. By 2010, how many single mothers are expected to file for bankruptcy?

This year [2005] more than 1 million women are expected to file for bankruptcy, outnumbering men by about 150,000 if trends hold.

Critics say that means the new U.S. bankruptcy law, which makes it harder for filers to expunge [remove] debts, is particularly onerous [troublesome] for women.

They expect the Oct. 17 [2005] law to saddle women with higher debts for longer periods and erode their economic security and ability to recover from financial crises not of their own doing.

"Filing for bankruptcy is the financial equivalent of going to a medical emergency room," said Karen Gross, president of the New York-based Coalition for Consumer Bankruptcy Debtor Education. "The new law significantly increases the barriers of getting in, the costs once inside and the hurdles of leaving."

New provisions of the law are designed to discourage filings under Chapter 7 of the U.S. Bankruptcy Code—which expunges debts—and steer more filers toward Chapter 13, under which they must repay at least some of their debts.

Higher Costs Are Bad News

Higher costs for filing bankruptcy under new provisions of the law are also bad news for women, say advocates, because women are less likely to have the savings to pay them.

One new provision of the law, for instance, requires bankruptcy attorneys to verify that they have investigated the debtor's information and believe it to be accurate. This added attorney time is expected to drive up filing costs, on average, by between $1,000 to $2,000. The actual filing fees with the court will also rise slightly along with the amount of time a lawyer will take to prepare a bankruptcy petition, said Howard Ehrenberg, a lawyer and Chapter 7 court-appointed bankruptcy trustee for the Central District of California.

In order to emerge from bankruptcy, filers must attend mandatory credit counseling and debtor education. While some of these courses are free, they can cost as much as $50 for a 90-minute session.

People may obtain a waiver of those fees if they are destitute but the new law makes it harder for filers to prove they are unable to pay.

In April [2005], a nationwide survey by Visa USA and the Consumer Federation of America found that 42 percent of women who responded had less than $500 in emergency savings, and 55 percent of women age 25 to 34 did not maintain an emergency savings account of at least $500.

Survivors Hurt by New Means Test

Also hurt will be filers whose domestic partners die suddenly because a new means test used to determine who is eligible for bankruptcy protection applies only to personal income, not household income, Ehrenberg said. This means that people who depended on a partner's income cannot show that loss. Since women are more likely to survive their husbands, this new "means test" will more likely affect them.

Gross said women's higher number of bankruptcy protection filings reflects a complex set of social barriers to financial security: lower earnings, less education about money and, often, sole responsibility for raising children.

By 2010, 1 in 6 single mothers is expected to file for bankruptcy.

"When people wonder why women are in more financial trouble, it's because they earn less, they live longer, they get

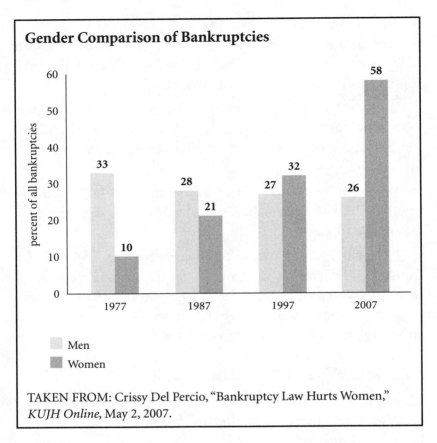

Gender Comparison of Bankruptcies

TAKEN FROM: Crissy Del Percio, "Bankruptcy Law Hurts Women," *KUJH Online*, May 2, 2007.

less support, they get sick, and they have huge obligations to their children," said Gross, a professor at New York Law School.

Jill Miller, president and CEO of Women Work!, a non-profit network in Washington, D.C., dedicated to women's economic security, said the vast majority of women who file for bankruptcy do so out of dire need. Miller was also honored as a Women's eNews 21 Leader for the 21st century in 2003.

"Nine of 10 times, women file for bankruptcy because they've lost their jobs, experienced a medical emergency or because of divorce or separation. The facts belie the myth that women are filing because they are irresponsible and frivolous spenders. That's just not the case."

Legislative Remedies

Advocates for women's economic security support a wide range of legislation that would help women become financially self-sufficient and protected from bankruptcy.

Those policies include paid family medical leave, benefits for part-time workers, increases in the federal minimum wage, and more funding for job training and education programs that help women advance in the workforce.

"There are many systemic issues, such as how bankruptcy affects women, which one should think about at the macro level," Gross said. "Most require seismic shifts. Some less seismic suggestions are to increase women's and girls' financial literacy levels, address their fear of numbers and improve their comfort levels with quantitative skills."

Miller criticized the bankruptcy law for focusing on a debtor's personal responsibility while ignoring credit card companies' marketing campaigns and exorbitant interest rates. "It does not address corporate responsibility," she said.

At the same time, advocates said the new law heightens the urgency of improving women's financial education.

"Girls are not being provided the kind of financial information and education that they need, either in school or while they are growing up," said Miller, whose organization conducted 15 focus groups on the subject of work-force challenges facing women in 12 states last summer. "Women told us they had to learn about finances by the seat of their pants."

Some women imperiled by the new law are not those seeking bankruptcy protection themselves. Instead, these are women who are struggling for back payments of child support from men facing financial pressures.

In the past, Miller said, filers were required to honor their child support obligations while being allowed to write off other forms of debt. But under a new provision of the law, credit card claims are put on equal footing with claims for back child support.

Now that women will have to compete with well-financed credit card companies for the assets of the same men who have filed for bankruptcy, Miller expects them to have a harder time collecting. Last year, $95 billion in child support went unpaid overall.

> *"Each interest rate rise makes such men*
> *more desperate."*

Men Are More Likely to Struggle with Finances than Women

Bob Ellis

In the following viewpoint, Bob Ellis, a regular contributor to The Sydney Morning Herald *and other Australian newspapers, argues that men commit suicide far more often than women because of economic struggles, including being deeply in debt. Citing statistics about men's suicide rates in Australia, Ellis asserts that when men can no longer live up to the image of breadwinner and must go in search of work that they often turn to suicide as a way of overcoming the mental and social strain.*

As you read, consider the following questions:

1. How often do Australian dairy farmers commit suicide?

2. Compared to women, how many more Australian men commit suicide each day?

3. How does Australia's suicide rate compare with the rest of the world?

For a while I stood at the train station, an hour perhaps, wondering which train I would jump in front of. There seemed no other way. Did I mean it? Or was it just a hypothetical dilemma, the sort we all have sometimes?

To be or not to be.

Two of the greatest plays, *Hamlet* and *Death of a Salesman*, are about thoughts of suicide, and one of the greatest films, *It's A Wonderful Life*, and one of the finer songs, *Waltzing Matilda*.

In my case they were brought on by (yes) a rise in interest rates; our mortgage payments had gone from $820 a week to $1,300 a week in six months; and this, in 1987, was hard for a freelance writer with an overworked wife and three children to contemplate. Was, in Hamlet's phrase, self-slaughter an option? It seemed so, or it seemed so to me for that hour on the train platform.

One Australian dairy farmer [commits] suicide every four days, Bob Katter [Australian federal politician] revealed in anguish in parliament last month [2008], some of them friends of his.

Each interest rate rise makes such men more desperate. Even selling the farm won't get them out of it; the drought and the ARB [Australian Reserve Bank] have seen to that.

A gun in the mouth, a pulled trigger, seems a better alternative. This may well be so.

In ancient Rome committing suicide was a way of sending a message to the Emperor: your dread regime, oh Caesar, has driven me to this. These days suicide bombing does much the same work: you infidels' foul presence on our holy ground has driven me to this, American scum. Please go away.

Young and mid-aged males are most of those who [commit] suicide, during high school exams, failed love affairs, unemployment, retrenchment, divorce, bankruptcy, small business ventures going bust.

The "Loser" Concept

Five Australian men [commit] suicide each day and only one woman. Why is this so?

Well, men have images of themselves, as conqueror, provider, breadwinner, football star, self-made billionaire, chick magnet, local hero, which, if they fail at, darken their mood. There are so many things they can fail at, so many contests they are in, so many medals they will not win, so many promises to keep, that the gun in the drawer comes to mind pretty frequently, or its equivalent.

How many deaths by car crash are witting acts of suicide by mid-aged males, self-slaughter? We will never know.

The American concept "loser" has a lot to do with it.

A loser is a forty-year-old man who is not a billionaire—or an Olympic gold medallist, or pitcher for the Red Sox, or CEO at Disney, or a Hollywood hunk getting ten million dollars a film. 98 percent of American men are losers, therefore, and can buy handguns easily on Main Street in any leafy town.

Sometimes from retrenchment to murder-suicide or marriage break-up to college massacre takes only a couple of days.

How many botched bank hold-ups are witting acts of self-slaughter, of topping oneself, of losing it altogether? We will also never know. How many suburban sieges, plane hijackings, deaths by alcoholic poisoning or medication overdose, knife fights in pubs after midnight?

Always, as in [Swedish director Ingmar] Bergman's *The Seventh Seal* the black-cowled tempter Death stalks you, the exhausted male, smiles behind your shoulder in the shaving mirror.

Many Lose Everything

Most men who have gone broke, lost their woman, lost their children, think of doing away with themselves. . . .

India's Debt-Ridden Farmers Committing Suicide

While India's economy surges forward on the crest of globalization, thousands of farmers are taking their own lives every year to escape mounting debt and an uncertain future. According to the National Crime Records Bureau, at least 87,567 farmers committed suicide between 2002 and 2006. In Maharashtra state, there were 4,453 suicides in 2006, the last year for which statistics were made available, an increase of 527 compared with 2005. Sharp increases have also been reported in Andhra Pradesh and Chhattisgarh states.

Jason Motlagh,
"India's Debt-Ridden Farmers Committing Suicide,"
San Francisco Chronicle, *March 23, 2008.*

In a film my wife Anne Brooksbank wrote, *Moving On*, about a farmer forced off the land in 1975, is the loyal wife's bleak line, "You spend your life tiptoeing around a man's pride." It resounds now still.

The women watch as the men crack up. They hide the whisky bottle. They hide the rifle. They join the prayer group. They make the begging phone calls. They investigate the necessary medication. They cop the odd belt in the face. They stand by their man. This is what women, or many women, do. They cope, they deal with the children, they rally round. They bury their egos and keep the show on the road.

But men are warriors in the end. They need the testing battles that will prove their worth or end their lives.

They are challenge-seeking animals, heat-seeking missiles, fools for pointless contest. They need the victory at darts, at pool, at horse-betting, marlin fishing, stock-market speculation that affirms them.

They need that struggle with the numbers which proves if they are losers, or if they are not.

"Going Where the Work Is"

Is economic rationalism a cause of male suicide? Of course it is.

Any change of address, any loss of job, any default in a mortgage payment, . . . any office downsizing that targets you or your lifestyle, is a sanity-threatening trauma, an ego-diminishing kick in the guts, a personal catastrophe.

Ask any unemployed male from Leeton, Cessnock, Elizabeth or Beaconsfield who is living elsewhere now and looking for work.

Anything that takes you away from your community, your siblings, your congregation, your local team, your grandchildren, your mates in the pub, your certainty of sexual relief is a suicide-inducement zone.

"Going where the work is" for most country town men, is the first paragraph of a suicide note to their extended family, the cousins and aunts and uncles they won't see much any more.

Does the ARB, then, increase the suicide rate in men? Of course it does; three or four times a year, it seems.

[Former Australian prime minister Paul John] Keating's fool smug phrase "The recession we had to have" really means, when decrypted, "The suicides we had to have". The able-bodied men we sacrifice to Moloch [ancient god requiring sacrifice] on an altar of burning bank-notes, and their wives and children thrown on the pyre as the flames increase.

[Historian] C. Northcote Parkinson once in an essay said a civilisation's success could be measured by adding up the suicide rate, the alcoholism rate, divorce rate, road death rate, cost of health care, number of college graduates, number of deaths in babyhood, average age at death, and so on.

By these means he unsurprisingly named the world-wide winner as Holland. But suicide he ranked very high in the red column of his numbering.

And Australia today has the second highest suicide rate in the world.

How are we doing?

We have the highest mortgage instalments in world history too. There may be a connection, oh my comrades, oh my fellow Australians, there really may, between an ARB that "fights inflation" by raising the cost of living (by $80 a week this fiscal year [2008] thus far) and the farmer Bob Katter knows who blows his brains out; there may just be a connection.

Periodical Bibliography

The following articles have been selected to supplement the diverse views presented in this chapter.

Laura Cohn	"Credit Advice You Can Trust," *Kiplinger's Personal Finance*, May 2009.
L. Gordon Crovitz	"Easy Credit and the Depression," *The Wall Street Journal*, May 4, 2009.
Darren Dahl	"Why Small Businesses Still Can't Borrow Money," *The New York Times*, May 7, 2009.
Charles Duhigg	"What Does Your Credit-Card Company Know About You?" *The New York Times Magazine*, May 17, 2009.
Tara Kalwarski	"Households Borrow Less, but Their Debt Barely Drops," *Business Week*, May 4, 2009.
Diane V. King	"Making Their Money," *Black Enterprise*, April 2009.
Ben Levisohn	"The Unemployment Effect," *BusinessWeek*, April 20, 2009.
Robert McNatt	"Tough Choices for Specialty Finance Companies," *BusinessWeek Online*, May 18, 2009.
Sarah Murnen	"Who's at Fault for Credit-Card Woes?" *The Christian Science Monitor*, May 9, 2009.
Sheryl Nance-Nash	"Hard Lessons in Home Economics," *Black Enterprise*, May 2009.
Kimberly Palmer	"The Fate of the Middle Class," *U.S. News & World Report*, March 1, 2009.
Yolanda Young	"Black Spending Ways Face Judgment Day," *USA Today*, May 8, 2009.

OPPOSING
VIEWPOINTS®
SERIES

CHAPTER 3

Does the U.S. Government Manage Debt Responsibly?

Chapter Preface

The U.S. government constantly walks a fine line between respecting free trade and capitalism by allowing companies to rise and fall at their own hand and getting involved when economic matters take on a national urgency. Occasionally, as in the case of the airline industry in 2001, the government assists companies in improving their economic situations. Referred to as a bailout, this strategy is usually implemented to avoid the crash of an entire industry. In the wake of the global financial downturn, the federal government made the decision to bail out the mortgage and auto industries as a means of preventing further economic failure. As with any multi-billion dollar decision, the government's bailouts, especially of the failing auto industry, have caused quite a bit of controversy.

In 2008 the government made the decision to help the auto industry move toward economic recovery after years of declining profits. The government invested billions of dollars in the so-called "Big Three" automakers: General Motors, Ford Motor Company, and Chrysler Group LLC. The decision was based on the idea that if these car companies failed, the effects to the national economy would be severe and far-reaching, leading to massive unemployment and even the potential failure of the banking industry. In support of the bailout, Jeffrey Sachs, director of the Earth Institute at Columbia University and the author of *Common Wealth: Economics for a Crowded Planet*, argued that the bailout was the only way to save an important part of the American economy. In a November 2008 article in *The Washington Post*, Sachs says, "Because of the impact on parts suppliers, the shutdown of one company would imperil domestic production across the board, and the jobs at risk include not only the 1 million in vehicle assembly and parts, but millions more that would be caught in the resulting cascade of failures."

Not everyone, however, was in favor of the bailout. Some opponents argue that it violates the principles of a free market economy in which businesses fail or succeed based on their own merit. According to Steve Chapman, a columnist and editorial writer for the *Chicago Tribune*, auto industry executives made poor decisions, and their companies should have to face the consequences. In an article that appeared on Townhall.com in September 2008, Chapman argues, "Saving companies from their bad gambles turns business into a game of 'profits for me, losses for you,' corroding the incentives that make capitalism so innovative and efficient." Others who spoke out against the bailout, noted that other industries, such as the steel industry, have not been bailed out and have failed.

It is a difficult balance for a government built on capitalism and a free market economy to make decisions about the future of its populace. It is clear that the fallout of the looming failure of the auto industry would have been catastrophic, but some people argued that the government should have allowed the failure to occur rather than making monetary advances that will force future generations of Americans to pay higher taxes and sacrifice goods and services provided by the government. On the other hand, as the authors in this chapter argue, the government believed that the bailout was the best way to manage debt responsibly.

| "A debt-based monetary system has a
lifespan-limiting Achilles' heel . . ."

The U.S. Economy Is Failing Because It Is Debt-Based

Steven Lachance

In the following viewpoint, financial translator Steven Lachance argues that an economy cannot survive long on a debt-based model. When there are no longer ways of covering debt, then economies in this situation have few choices to survive. He explains that as debt is created through loans, a financial obligation that goes beyond the original loan amount is created through interest charges. Unfortunately, the only way that both payments can be paid is if more debt is taken on, which creates a cycle of what amounts to an economy based on paper and not on actual wealth.

As you read, consider the following questions:

1. Between 1987 and 2005, how much has the total credit market debt grown?

2. How was the $3 trillion dollars that the United States incurred in debt in 2005 used by the government and consumers?

3. What occurred on June 16, 2003?

Most know debt is a by-product of the finance-centered US economic model. Few, however, are familiar with how much debt the US credit system creates, let alone the implications. The upshot is financial decision making based on mainstream herding and hesitancy to take essential steps to preserve personal wealth.

Where Does Debt Come From?

According to the most recent Flow of Funds report from the Federal Reserve, total credit market debt (TCMD) expanded by $799 billion in the third quarter of 2005. At this rate, debt growth for a single year is $3 trillion, or 50% greater than total US industrial production. Since 1987, the year Alan Greenspan became chairman of the Federal Reserve Board, TCMD has more than tripled, from $13 trillion to $40 trillion, and now accounts for well over 300% of GDP [gross domestic product]. This debt growth is without precedent by any relative or absolute measure, evidence that the US has experienced a debt bubble.

Traditionally, savings finance debt. As the US savings rate has been anemic [weak] for years, many establishment economists, Ben Bernanke among them, have claimed that US debt growth is supported by the inflow of surplus savings from abroad—the global savings glut thesis. Net purchases of US debt by foreign interests, though, are less than $1 trillion per year, far short of annual debt growth of $3 trillion. Some commentators are quick to point a finger at the Fed [Federal Reserve Board]; it's printing money they say. This too misses the mark. As of 9 December [2005], Fed credit was up just 3.5% YoY [year over year] and the combined balance sheet of the 12 Federal Reserve Banks is barely $1 trillion.

The pump for the epic American debt bubble is neither foreign savings nor the Fed. For the $27 trillion of debt created during his tenure, Alan Greenspan can thank the private sector and the government-sponsored enterprises (GSEs). The Fed may be negligent for losing control of the credit system, but it is not directly responsible for what has occurred since. The GSEs' combined book of business, for instance, dwarfs the Fed balance sheet at nearly $3 trillion. Anchored by the money center banks, a vast constellation of financial entities, including mortgage lenders, consumer credit firms, and the financial arms of industrial enterprises, has blossomed to do with a vengeance what the Fed itself would not; create a seemingly unlimited quantity of debt out of thin air through loan origination.

How Does Debt End?

Debt is self-liquidating when used to generate future income, from which interest is serviced and principal repaid. Used for any other purpose, it is non-self-liquidating and results in payment obligations with no countervailing source of income. Of the $3 trillion in debt created this year [2005], households used about 50% for mortgages and consumer loans, governments 25%, and companies 25%. Only companies incur self-liquidating debt, so at least 75%, or $2.25 trillion, of the debt has produced a future burden rather than an income stream. Companies, though, are no white knights. They have mostly used their $750 billion of the debt pie for purposes other than capital investment, namely to cover unfunded liabilities and buyback shares they liberally printed to reward management in the first place. The US is, thus, at or close to a situation whereby the percentage of debt financed by domestic savings is zero and the percentage of non-self-liquating debt is one hundred.

A debt-based monetary system has a lifespan-limiting Achilles' heel: as debt is created through loan origination, an obligation above and beyond this sum is also created in the form of interest. As a result, there can never be enough money

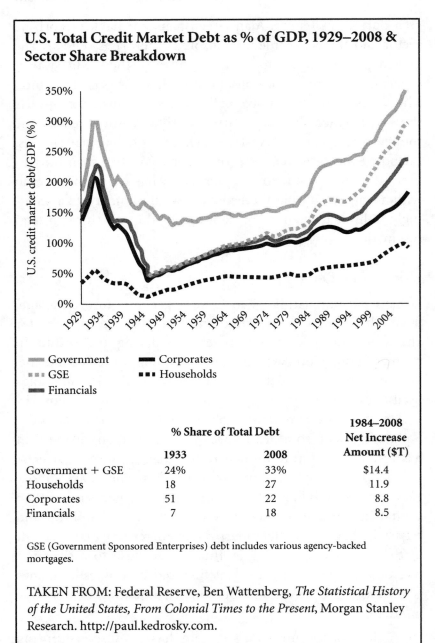

U.S. Total Credit Market Debt as % of GDP, 1929–2008 & Sector Share Breakdown

Legend:
— Government — Corporates
∙∙∙ GSE ∙∙∙ Households
— Financials

	% Share of Total Debt		1984–2008 Net Increase Amount ($T)
	1933	2008	
Government + GSE	24%	33%	$14.4
Households	18	27	11.9
Corporates	51	22	8.8
Financials	7	18	8.5

GSE (Government Sponsored Enterprises) debt includes various agency-backed mortgages.

TAKEN FROM: Federal Reserve, Ben Wattenberg, *The Statistical History of the United States, From Colonial Times to the Present,* Morgan Stanley Research. http://paul.kedrosky.com.

to repay principal and pay interest unless debt is continually expanded. Debt-based monetary systems do not work in reverse, nor can they stand still without a liquidity buffer in the form of savings or a current account surplus.

When debt grows faster than the economy, the burden of interest is bearable only so long as the rate of interest is falling. When the rate of interest reverses course, interest charges start rising faster than debt growth. This point was reached on 16 June 2003, the day the yield on the benchmark 10-year Treasury bottomed at 3.09%. Since then, debt grew from $32 trillion to $40 trillion, an increase of 25%. During the same period, annual interest charges rose by over 50%, from $1.28 trillion ($32 trillion at the prevailing average interest rate for debtors of 4%) to $2.0 trillion ($40 trillion at 5%). When interest charges exceed debt growth, debtors at the margin are unable to service their debt. They must begin liquidating.

Dipping into savings or running a current account surplus can offset liquidation for a time. The greater the pool of savings and the current account surplus, the longer an economy can endure liquidation at the margin without experiencing cascading cross-defaults [when a default on one debt obligation results in a default on another debt obligation]. The US in the early 1930s and Japan in the early 1990s had such a liquidity buffer. In both cases, mobilizing domestic savings to increase government debt reversed the decline in total debt outstanding in two to three years and interest rates stayed low because savings financed the new debt. As a result, interest charges no longer exceeded debt growth and the need for marginal debtors to liquidate disappeared.

The US is now in a fundamentally different position than it was in 1930 or Japan was in 1990. Aside from a dearth of domestic savings, its vulnerability is compounded by a current account deficit. There is no buffer and no margin for error. Thus, when interest charges, now $2 trillion per year and accelerating, overtake annual debt growth, now $3 trillion and decelerating, liquidation will immediately trigger cascading cross-defaults. Without domestic savings to mobilize, the Fed cannot facilitate the expansion of government debt to fill the breach and simultaneously hold down interest rates. It cannot win the battle to keep debt growth greater than interest charges, the precondition for the viability of a debt-based monetary system. Once started, cascading cross-defaults consume all debt within an economy. The Fed has only two options: institute a new monetary system with a new currency or return monetary authority to the market and shut down.

> *"The pitiful truth is that, if you are in financial distress, you are flashing dollar signs at credit issuers."*

The U.S. Economy Is Failing Because It Is Credit-Based

Andrew Leonard

Andrew Leonard is a senior technology writer for Salon.com and a contributing writer for Wired Magazine. *In the following viewpoint, he argues that the U.S. economy is in distress in part because of predatory lending, which occurs when financial institutions offer high-risk borrowers money at a high premium. Consumers who have recently filed bankruptcy are especially targeted by these lenders because they cannot file again for many years. Although many Americans believe that people who file bankruptcy are not careful at managing their finances, Leonard asserts that many filers have struggled with personal and financial tragedies beyond their control.*

As you read, consider the following questions:

1. According to a report by the Consumer Bankruptcy Project, what percentage of borrowers were solicited by creditors just a year after filing bankruptcy?

2. What are attractive cash flows?

3. According to Katherine Porter, what are the main reasons that consumers file bankruptcy?

No discussion of credit woes in the American economy is complete without a raging flame war between those who believe government should prevent "predatory" lenders from taking unfair advantage of borrowers, and those who believe that borrowers who can't pay what they owe are deadbeats who deserve to be publicly mocked, if not shackled and thrown directly into debtors' prison.

Echoes of this hallowed clash can be heard in the ongoing debate over what to do with all those subprime mortgage borrowers currently experiencing the joys of resetting ARMs [adjustable rate mortgages] and receiving foreclosure notices in their mail. Let 'em rot in a dungeon built from their own stupidity, cry those who always pay their credit card bills on time and never fail to read the fine print. Most of 'em are scammers who knowingly abused the system, they say. Either that, or recklessly foolish to the point where they deserve nothing less than a night in the stockade.

"Something Had to Be Done"

If you happened to follow the tos and fros in the debate over the new federal bankruptcy law passed in 2005, which made it much harder for Americans to declare personal bankruptcy, you will no doubt find this rhetoric familiar. The credit industry, which lobbied hard for bankruptcy "reform," framed the issue as one in which something had to be done about all those immoral people running up credit card bills that they knew they wouldn't be able to pay back. And why not? They could always escape their debts by declaring bankruptcy.

Never mind that there was next to zero empirical data supporting this argument. The credit industry won the day. Some day soon, now that Americans are once again running up their credit card bills as they try to find a way to keep afloat without the help of magically appreciating home prices, we may find out exactly how smart this "reform" will turn out to be. In the meantime, it might be useful to go back and review exactly how the credit card industry treated, *in practice*, Americans who had already declared bankruptcy, even as it was castigating them, in rhetoric, as wastrels and scoundrels.

Surprise! Bankrupt Americans get all kinds of love from the credit industry. According to data compiled and analyzed by Katherine Porter, a law professor at the University of Iowa, in the superb "Bankrupt Profits: The Credit Industry's Business Model for Post-Bankruptcy Lending":

> ... Creditors repeatedly solicit debtors to borrow after bankruptcy. Families receive dozens of offers for new credit in each month immediately after their bankruptcy discharge. Some offers specifically target these families based on their recent financial problems, using bankruptcy as an advertising lure. Other credit offers emanate from the very same lenders that the families could not repay before bankruptcy. While not every lender will accept a "profligate" [wasteful] bankrupt as a customer, debtors report being overwhelmed after bankruptcy with a variety of credit solicitations from many sources. Lenders offer families most types of secured and unsecured loans.

Survey data compiled by the Consumer Bankruptcy Project reveals:

- Just one year after bankruptcy, 96.1 percent of debtors were recipients of credit solicitations.

- One year post-bankruptcy, these families reported that creditors sent them an average of more than fourteen credit offers per month.

- Industry researchers report that the average American gets six credit offers each month.

Identifying Predatory Lending

The term "predatory lending" covers a potentially broad range of behavior and does not lend itself to a concise or comprehensive definition. However, predatory lending typically involves at least one, and perhaps all three of the following elements:

- making unaffordable loans based on the assets of the borrower, rather than on the borrower's ability to repay an obligation ("asset-based lending")

- inducing a borrower to refinance a loan repeatedly in order to charge high points and fees each time the loan is refinanced ("loan flipping")

- engaging in fraud or deception to conceal the true nature of the loan obligation from an unsuspecting or unsophisticated borrower.

State of New Jersey Department of Banking & Insurance,
"Predatory Lending—What Consumers Should Know,"
April 12, 2009. www.state.nj.us.

- A vast majority of debtors had received credit solicitations that specifically mentioned their bankruptcy. Nearly 88 percent of debtors reported that lenders had referenced the debtor's bankruptcy in their credit marketing.

Why? Why would a credit industry that was lobbying Congress to protect it from being abused engage in such willful self-flagellation?

In the first year after filing, many families face financial difficulty and must cope with declining or stagnant incomes.

People in financial distress are more likely to have revolving accounts, to have exceeded their credit limit, and to use cash advances (which carry a higher interest rate), creating what some researchers have termed "attractive cash flows."

These families may be slow to pay; they may make only small payments; they may incur huge fees; and their balances may negatively amortize. But they cannot seek bankruptcy relief. It is precisely this constellation of features that makes post-bankruptcy families particularly profitable for lenders.

Bankruptcy as a Last Resort

The pitiful truth is that, if you are in financial distress, you are flashing dollar signs at credit issuers.

According to Porter, decades of research indicate that "job problems, illness/injury or family break-up were pandemic in the bankrupt population." In other words, people tend to declare bankruptcy because traumatic financial events force them to do so, not because it was their plan all along. And the credit industry knows that.

> The strong overall pattern of credit offers to bankruptcy debtors suggests that creditors themselves reject a view of bankruptcy filers as either immoral individuals who chronically fail to honor their obligations or as strategic actors who are apt to abuse legal protections to avoid debts.

And where do we end up?

> If lenders' intense solicitation of such customers indeed is driven by these families' propensity to pay late, go over the limit, and revolve large balances, society may wish to prohibit or constrain such lending.

Well, that's what a *civilized* society might wish to do. What the United States will ultimately decide is another question.

> "As a society, Americans have always
> encouraged economic activity through
> the extensive use of credit."

The U.S. Government
Should Encourage People
to Take on New Debt

Nathalie Martin

In the following viewpoint, Nathalie Martin, a law professor at the University of New Mexico, argues that debt forgiveness practices in the United States help the economy flourish. By allowing individuals and small businesses to fail, these practices give entrepreneurs the courage to take chances. The United States has a history of successful business titans who at one time failed. Encouraging consumers to take on new debt energizes the economy.

As you read, consider the following questions:

1. What are the two main types of bankruptcy?

2. Name three American businessmen whose early attempts at business failed.

3. From what sources do many new entrepreneurs acquire money for start-up costs?

Nathalie Martin, "American Bankruptcy Laws Encourage Risk-Taking and Entrepreneurship," *eJournal USA: Economic Perspectives*, January 1, 2006.

The United States relies heavily on the use of credit by both individuals and businesses to fuel its economy. The country also has forgiving bankruptcy laws that protect individuals and businesses if they become financially insolvent. As such, these laws support capitalism and the growth of small businesses by encouraging people to take business risks.

For individuals, there are two main types of bankruptcy:

- One type, known as Chapter 7, allows people in financial trouble to "discharge"—be forgiven for—most debts for which there is no collateral (security). This type of bankruptcy does not help a person become current with secured debts, where the borrower has pledged some form of collateral, such as property.

- The second type, known as Chapter 13, allows people in financial trouble to pay back a portion of their debts through a payment plan extending over three to five years. At the end of the period, assuming the debtor has contributed all of his or her disposable income to the payment plan, the remaining debts are forgiven. This type can be used to pay off past-due secured debt and thus keep the collateral.

For businesses, the law is a bit different. Some can stay in business under Chapter 11 while they reorganize their debts. Thus, unlike most bankruptcy systems around the world, U.S. laws allow a bankrupt company to continue in operation, with the same management, while it tries to restructure its debts. In other words, typically, no trustee or custodian is appointed. Some people think this system, known as a debtor-in-possession system, promotes economic and job growth because more companies remain in business and their assets are protected. Businesses can also simply liquidate their assets under Chapter 7 and use the sale proceeds to pay creditors.

The Underlying Philosophy

The American economy is extremely vibrant and active. The more activity in the economy, the stronger the economy will be. The U.S. regulatory structure has been developed to encourage people to create businesses, with the hope that they will succeed, hire employees, pay taxes, and otherwise improve the economy as a whole. We acknowledge that in the process, some businesses will fail. Thus, as a culture, we value a person's willingness to risk his or her job and money (and borrowed money, too) for the chance to succeed.

These ideas are not new. As a society, Americans have always encouraged economic activity through the extensive use of credit. As early as the 1700s, when the U.S. economy was competing with much more developed European economies, it grew faster than anyone could have imagined and quickly became the world's largest economy.

The extensive use of credit in the early U.S. economy was unique in the world, with some people being paid for goods and supplies months and even years after the credit was granted. This allowed people to start businesses without much money in their pockets. The availability of credit caused economic activity to soar, and a strong credit-based economy was born.

Having this much credit in the system had a downside as well. Some of the businesses failed. Even so, America was friendly to the capitalist spirit since its goal was to encourage people to take risks in business in order to fuel its young economy. A legal culture of tolerance of nonpayment developed that encouraged people to continue entrepreneurial pursuits, even if they had failed before.

The relative lenience of American bankruptcy law, as compared to the law on the European continent, shocked some people, including French philosopher Alexis de Tocqueville, who, in the early 1800s, commented on the "strange indulgence" shown to bankrupt companies in the American union.

He claimed that in this respect, "the Americans differ not only from the nations of Europe, but from all the commercial nations of our time."

Modern Bankruptcy Laws in Practice

If a business in the United States fails, the individual undertaking it can move on with his or her life without living in shame or total poverty. This is more than just a nice theory.

Many of America's most successful businessmen failed in early business endeavors, including ketchup magnate John Henry Heinz, Henry Ford of Ford Motor Company, and Phineas Barnum, who founded the American circus. All of these men eventually became very rich, in part because they were given a chance to try a business, fail, and start over.

Small businesses in the United States are the driving force behind the economy, employing more people than do huge, multinational companies. The credit system and its counterpart, the bankruptcy system, clearly support small businesses and entrepreneurship. Yet the sheer amount of credit available in the United States is daunting by global standards, with many average Americans able to get credit of $50,000 or more from bank loans, credit cards, and other sources, even without posting collateral. Many new entrepreneurs start their businesses with money from these sources.

Many people outside the United States find the U.S. bankruptcy laws odd, in part because they are so different from the laws in their own countries. Debt is not easily forgiven in most parts of the world, and there often is a stigma associated with financial failure. In many parts of Europe, any business failure is viewed as an embarrassment, even if you work for someone else's business and it fails. Someone associated with a business failure may even have trouble finding another job. In some parts of the world, such as Japan, my research has found that the stigma from financial failure is strong enough to lead people to commit suicide.

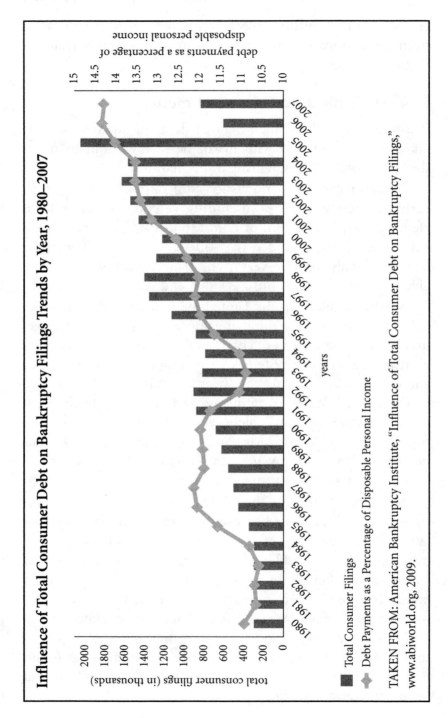

Influence of Total Consumer Debt on Bankruptcy Filings Trends by Year, 1980–2007

■ Total Consumer Filings

◆ Debt Payments as a Percentage of Disposable Personal Income

TAKEN FROM: American Bankruptcy Institute, "Influence of Total Consumer Debt on Bankruptcy Filings," www.abiworld.org, 2009.

Nevertheless, other countries—including Japan, Italy, France, the United Kingdom, and Germany—are starting to make their own laws more forgiving in order to promote entrepreneurialism and to fuel more active economies. In some places, lawmakers believe that a more forgiving bankruptcy system will save assets and fuel economies that are not growing quickly. Deflationary Japan is one example of a country attempting to use more forgiving bankruptcy laws to create more borrowing and more economic activity. Since most of these laws are quite new, it is not yet clear whether these changes will help promote small-business development. Sometimes, cultural factors might also keep people from availing themselves of these new, more forgiving laws.

There is much less stigma associated with a failed business in the United States. Some prospective employers might even consider an employee from a failed company to be more valuable because of the lessons learned at the prior job. Moreover, research shows that many U.S. owners who do well in business have failed in prior business ventures. The ability to start over is what makes some Americans willing to take risks in business, which can be good for the overall economy. The extensive availability of credit is also very helpful for the new entrepreneur.

The Economic Role of Consumer Debt

In addition to the debt Americans take on to start businesses, they also use credit to buy consumer items such as homes, cars, furniture, and clothing. Americans use credit cards rather than cash more frequently than people in other parts of the world. As a group, they also buy more consumer goods, even more than people living in other rich countries such as Japan and Canada. Maintaining a high level of consumer spending is great for the American economy, particularly when business spending is down.

However, U.S. bankruptcy laws are not as forgiving as they are for business for those individual consumers who use credit extensively to buy consumer goods. There is a strong correlation between consumer debt and financial failure, and bankruptcy resulting from consumer spending.

Moreover, individuals who overextend themselves financially on consumer goods will find it harder to discharge their debts. This is the result of a recent change in U.S. consumer bankruptcy laws designed to reign in consumer spending.

Fueling an active economy in the United States can be seen almost as a civic duty. Taking on credit risks to start a business can provide great financial rewards. If the business does well, the entrepreneur will flourish. If it fails, the person will get a second chance. Taking on extensive consumer debt carries the same risks with almost none of the rewards.

> *"Most of the US population continues destructive, over-consuming behaviors that harm all of us."*

The U.S. Government Should Discourage Excessive Consumption

Shepherd Bliss

Shepherd Bliss is a psychology professor at Sonoma State University in California. In the following viewpoint, he argues that the U.S. economy is in such dire straits partly because of excessive consumer credit. The destruction of the environment, elevated gasoline prices, and the fall of the housing market are all part of a larger system of disorder that are rooted in a common attitude toward overconsumption. Bliss encourages Americans to prepare for the worst.

As you read, consider the following questions:

1. Name at least three major American institutions that are in financial crisis.

Shepherd Bliss, "US Economy—Recession, Depression, or Collapse?" CommonDreams .org, November 14, 2007. Copyright © 2007 Shepherd Bliss. Reproduced by permission of the author.

2. According to "The Hidden Costs of the Iraq War," as of the end of 2007, how much debt has the U.S. government accrued in fighting the war in Iraq?

3. What are three ways Americans can respond to the worsening economic situation?

"For Consumers, the Hits Keep Coming" a recent banner headline in *The New York Times*-owned daily newspaper here in Northern California reports. The article misses the main points. If we continue to understand ourselves as primarily passive consumers, rather than as active citizens, the US economy will enter at least a recession, probably a depression, and possibly a collapse. Even our republic is at risk.

Rampant consumption, our addiction to growth, and our failure to accept limits to growth damage us. The headline beneath the banner—"Cleanup Response Criticized"—reveals one of the saddest results. We are not adequately cleaning up the San Francisco Bay after a recent oil spill. Many other aspects of our environment need cleaning up. Without a healthy natural environment and climate conducive to humans, no economy can endure. Overconsumption drives the increasingly extreme and chaotic climate.

We have contaminated our air and waterways, clear-cut our forests, and our inner cities are dying. The pollution of such natural resources often precedes economic and societal collapses.

Deeper, Systematic Causes

I appreciate the *Press Democrat* for recently reporting the emerging economic trends in numerous articles. What I miss is more analysis, connecting the dots and providing context. The shrinking dollar, soaring gas prices, housing slump and stock market fall, though inconvenient, are not the biggest threats to the economy. These are symptoms caused by deeper systemic problems. We need to learn from these events and discover how to build more sustainable societies. Otherwise, these "hits" are likely to increase and spread.

We need to quickly evolve from our destructive individual consumption patterns that damage not only the economy but the earth itself. We need to consider their many negative impacts and work together as active citizens concerned with the whole economy and the environment on which it is dependent.

Look around. Things are falling down and apart in the US, including cities like New Orleans, the Minneapolis bridge, and the Twin Towers. An increasing number of high-level government officials—like Karl Rove and Alberto Gonzales—have been forced out of office. The cuts are likely to go deeper. One can try to ignore, deny, or seek revenge for these events, all of which invite more disasters. Prudent planning would be a better alternative. These are not isolated events but point to systemic causes.

These are more than the "economic cycle of advance and retreat" that the Nov. 10 [2007] article reports. It is not just "things (that) have come together in the last 10 days." The US's false economy has been de-stabilizing for years and is now reaching a more degraded stage. We have become vulnerable to a variety of "hits" and should expect even more. Our economy has been described by some as a "house of cards," which is likely to fall. An unraveling is occurring, creating a time of great uncertainty and fear.

Many major American institutions are in crisis, including health care, religion, transportation, political systems, energy, and education.

The Iron Curtain came down and the Berlin Wall seemed to suddenly fall, as did the Soviet Union. The US economy may suddenly fail.

"A New Doom and Gloom Will Open Here." Cartoom by Lindsay Foyle. www.Cartoon Stock.com.

Revealing the Truth

Protecting markets and "consumers" from the truth of how bad our economic reality is will backfire. We do not need to "panic." But citizens do need accurate news and analysis to get ready for the potential of a radically diminished economy. We are living in a time of unprecedented planetary crisis. People need to prepare physically and psychologically for massive changes.

It is not enough to write about a "silver lining" and report the perilous optimism of an economist wishing that "hopefully this week is not a microcosm of where we will be a year from now." We need more than false hope to get us through the coming hard times.

Most of the US population continues destructive, over-consuming behaviors that harm all of us. We are not merely victims of the problems; we cause them. We cannot merely blame outside "terrorists."

Among the facts left out of recent articles in the mainstream press on the declining US economy is the Iraq War. With so many resources dedicated to war-making, dealing with events like [Hurricane] Katrina and cleaning up oil spills are more difficult.

"The Hidden Costs of the Iraq War" is a congressional report recently released. It states that the economic costs to the US of the wars in Iraq and Afghanistan are already around $1.5 trillion. For the average US family of four that is more than $20,000.

We are experiencing more than what headlines describe as a "slowdown." It could be a "meltdown." We might be approaching what James Howard Kunstler describes in his book *The Long Emergency* as "catastrophe."

Preparing for Disaster

Santa Rosa author Richard Heinberg's *Peak Everything* describes our situation well. *Waking Up to the Century of Declines* he sub-titles this new book. This sounds like bad news, but when we face changes early enough, we have more opportunities to cope with them and transform them into opportunities.

Helpful responses include reducing our consumption, accepting that we are contracting, and understanding ourselves as citizens able to take action, rather than as merely passive consumers who can only react. Citizen activism is what we most need at this point in history.

Humans can be far more than objects whose purpose is to buy, shop, spend, and grow the economy. We are threatened more by our own behavior than by any outside terrorists.

That which Heinberg and other Peak Oil theorists have been predicting for years seems to be entering its next stage. With the supply of petroleum and other fossil fuels diminishing and the demand for them increasing—especially from rapidly industrializing China and India—we are moving toward a radically worsened US economy.

When the mainstream press fails to report news and offer analyses that a large number of people are aware of, we can turn to citizen journalists on the Web. The mainstream press is losing readers because it no longer adequately investigates and reports some of the important stories. Fortunately, we now have other places to go to be informed and educated.

"Closing the 'Collapse Gap': The USSR Was Better Prepared for Collapse than the US" was published by the authoritative www.energybulletin.net. A Russian, Dmitry Orlov, who now lives in the US, wrote, "The US economy is poised to perform something like a disappearing act." Orlov compares the "two 20th century superpowers." . . .

Orlov examines the arms race, the space race, the jails race, and the "Hated Evil Empire Race." He concludes that "many of the problems that sunk the Soviet Union are now endangering the US." So we should "expect shortages of fuel, food, medicine, and countless consumer items, outages of electricity, gas, and water." If we plan for such possibilities now, we will be better able to deal with them.

Though Orlov details the threats to the US economy, he and his editors at Energy Bulletin remain optimistic. Orlov writes about the possibilities for an expansion of "enlightenment, fulfillment, and freedom" during times of collapse. Russia, after all, did recover. It may be more difficult for the US.

Useful Responses

Helpful responses include strengthening local economies, being less dependent upon globalization, outside corporations and things distant, and knowing and preserving the sources of the basics—such as food and water. "There are many things we can do to navigate down and around" our problems, Heinberg writes, "so as to enhance human sanity and security and happiness."

Canada is one of the many countries whose citizens are ahead of the US in prudent planning for pending crises caused by extreme climate, Peak Oil, and related matters. . . .

Too many Americans selfishly believe that they have a God-given right to consume whatever their wealth can purchase, without regard to the consequences to other people and the earth. They take, rather than give, even the natural resources of other peoples. As a farmer, I know that you reap what you sow and that chickens come home to roost.

Our economy is paying and will continue to pay the consequences of over-consumption and the over-purchasing of people reaching beyond their resources that characterized the housing market. We have been greedy. There are limits to growth and those limits are crashing in on us.

Yet many piles of rubble have been rebuilt—often more beautiful than before they fell. Phoenixes have risen from the ashes before. Yet our future is uncertain, without guarantees.

It is time to think and write about more than the probability of a recession and consider the real possibility of a depression or even collapse. Then people can get ready, be active citizens, and prepare their personal, social, and political responses. We must do this together.

| "The capitalists have extracted billions in profits and managed to leave the exploited nations hundreds of billions in debt."

The United States Exploits Borrowing by Developing Countries

Saul Kanowitz

Saul Kanowitz is a contributing writer for InFocus News, *the largest Muslim newspaper in California. In the following viewpoint, he argues that the U.S. government causes more problems than it solves when it works with African governments on expanding oil production. The costs of drilling, barreling, and shipping are beyond the budgets of most African nations, so the U.S. government loans them the operating costs. Unfortunately, this business arrangement does not help the economies of the African nations because in the end they are in debt to the U.S. government.*

As you read, consider the following questions:

1. Which African country is the largest producer of oil on the continent?

Saul Kanowitz, "Pentagon Targets Africa in New Drive for Oil," *Socialism and Liberation*, September 1, 2005. Reproduced by permission.

2. Since 1992 what percentage of all World Bank oil extraction projects have been export-oriented?

3. How much oil do the Gulf of Guinea states produce each day?

Before July's [2005] G8 [Group of Eight developed countries] summit in Scotland, the seven leading imperialist countries along with Russia announced with great fanfare a debt relief program that will "benefit" 23 African countries whose foreign debt is over $50 billion. The big-business press lauded this development as "historic," claiming the program "fulfilled a decades-old dream of anti-poverty activists."

However, an event with far greater implications for the people of Africa happened at the same time: the U.S. military sent a ship to the Gulf of Guinea to "train West African nations to combat threats including terrorism, drug trafficking and petroleum theft." This did not make a splash in the capitalist press, but U.S. imperialism's strategists understand its importance—oil.

The discovery of new oil resources in sub-Saharan Africa in recent years, particularly in the Gulf of Guinea, has intensified U.S. interests in the region. African oil has taken on greater significance in the U.S. drive to control the global economy.

Taking resources from Africa and exploiting its people is nothing new for the United States or other imperialist powers. The brutal legacy of the trans-Atlantic slave trade, later followed by numerous U.S. interventions, has haunted the continent's people for over four centuries.

From the Congress of Berlin in 1884 to the present, imperialist rulers have always viewed the vast human and natural resources of Africa as "theirs." Racist ideologies like the "white man's burden" and "manifest destiny" have been used by capitalists to justify genocide, the rape of natural resources, and enslaving tens of millions of Africans. As noted Pan-Africanist

George Padmore stated in 1936, "The Black man certainly has to pay dear for carrying the white man's burden."

A modern-day manifestation of these ideologies was articulated by U.S. policy makers at a 2002 conference in Washington, D.C., entitled, "African Oil: A Priority for U.S. National Security and African Development." At the conference, Walter Kansteiner, former assistant secretary of state for African affairs, declared: "It is undeniable that this [oil] has become of national strategic interest to us."

The U.S. government's fundamental goal in Africa is the same as the colonial plunderers who came before it—extract massive profits to enrich big banks and corporations. The welfare of Africa's people doesn't factor into the equation.

Underdevelopment and Oil

As with gold, diamonds and other valuable minerals, the discovery of oil in an imperialist-dominated world has not improved living standards for the vast majority of working and poor Africans.

Huge sums of money are required to invest in the machinery and technology to extract oil from the ground or within a nation's shoreline. Most African countries don't have enough money on demand; nor do they have the necessary technology because of the imperialists' deliberate policies to keep Africa poor and needy. For now, they need a cheap source of raw materials and labor. Additionally, the imperialists, led by the United States, want African countries to rely on them for development and technological gain.

This relationship has opened the door for U.S.-owned petroleum companies, like ChevronTexaco, to go into oil-rich African countries and begin mechanized oil extraction primarily for their own gain.

The development of the oil industry in Nigeria is an example of how capitalism continues to underdevelop Africa. Nigeria is the largest producer of oil on the continent. It currently provides 10 percent of U.S. oil imports—1.5 million barrels a day. Since 1965, Nigeria's net oil revenues total nearly $350 billion.

However, Nigeria's people are generally very poor. In 1970, the per capita gross domestic product [GDP] was $1,113. In 2004, the per capita GDP fell to $1,000. Over the same 34 years while Nigeria's per capita GDP fell, oil revenues increased tenfold. The benefits accrued almost solely to bourgeois owners in Nigeria. Nigeria is a class society. The Nigerian capitalist class is partners with the U.S. and European capitalists in the exploitation of the country.

In spite of the creation of this wealth, Nigeria has sunk further into debt. In 1970, Nigeria's debt was one billion dollars. Today, Nigeria owes imperialist banks more than $30 billion.

The accumulation of oil wealth by one percent of the population and the massive increase in Nigeria's foreign debt are the consequences of Nigeria's place in the world capitalist economy. The World Bank and the IMF [International Monetary Fund], working through the Nigerian capitalist elite and the government, have provided loans "by stipulation," which are necessary to fund drilling, extraction and oil processing. These stipulations prioritized oil exporting over domestic development. Since 1992, 82 percent of all oil extraction projects funded by the World Bank have been export-oriented.

People Fight Back

Oil is becoming increasingly important not only in Nigeria but to all of Africa in the global economic market. Daily oil production by the Gulf of Guinea states (Nigeria, Congo, Gabon, Cameroon and Equatorial Guinea) is over 4.5 million barrels. The total is more than Iran, Saudi Arabia or Venezuela produces individually. The top two U.S. oil companies, ChevronTexaco and ExxonMobil, plan to invest $70 billion in oil

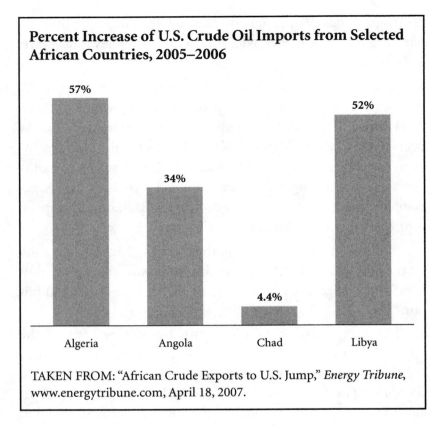

Percent Increase of U.S. Crude Oil Imports from Selected African Countries, 2005–2006

TAKEN FROM: "African Crude Exports to U.S. Jump," *Energy Tribune*, www.energytribune.com, April 18, 2007.

production over the next five to ten years in the Gulf of Guinea, according to the July 25 [2005] *Chinese People's Daily*.

In order to protect U.S. corporations' profits and capital investments, the Pentagon is moving into the Gulf. U.S. Special Forces recently have been sent to Chad, Mali and Nigeria as part of a program called the Pan Sahel Initiative, for the purpose of counter-terrorism training. The Pentagon is considering the island of São Tomé and Príncipe, in the heart of the Gulf, as a candidate for a permanent military base, according to the July 25 [2005] issue of Cuba's *Granma*.

But the uninterrupted exploitation of the peoples and resources of Africa does not guarantee future stability for the imperialists.

In 2002 and 2003, hundreds of Nigerian women organized against Shell and ChevronTexaco. They occupied terminals, airstrips, docks and stores in protest of massive exploitation and terrible living standards. After a protracted struggle, the women achieved many of their demands: jobs, schools, scholarships, hospitals, water, electricity and protection of the environment. The actions disrupted the production of about 450,000 barrels of crude oil each day.

A general strike in 2003 shut down businesses in the capital, Lagos, and several other cities for eight days. The police killed 11 people in response. In June and October 2004, the oil workers' unions conducted strikes over gasoline price increases.

The long history of economic exploitation and domination by foreign capital has impoverished much of the African continent. The capitalists have extracted billions in profits and managed to leave the exploited nations hundreds of billions in debt.

In 1867, Karl Marx described the birth of capitalism as "dripping from head to foot, from every pore, with blood and dirt." He wrote this to describe the genocidal method by which the economies of the European colonizing countries developed at the expense of the people oppressed by colonialism. Oil production and the attendant debt suffered by oil-producing countries is the modern continuation of this policy. This is especially true in Africa.

> *"They come to depend on that aid just like those on welfare and use it to enjoy a slightly higher standard of living than they can actually afford."*

The United States Has Become Overly Indebted by Lending Money to Developing Countries

J.R. Dieckmann

J.R. Dieckmann is the editor of GreatAmericanJournal.com and his writing has appeared in conservative publications, including The Conservative Voice *and* Real Clear Politics. *In the following viewpoint, he argues that the United States has such a high standard of living because of the many sacrifices that its citizens have made to ensure a free market economy. Other nations have not developed in the same way. It is not the job of the U.S. government or its people to loan or give money to other nations. Instead, those countries must perish or flourish on their own.*

J.R. Dieckmann, "Is Foreign Aid Contributing to World Poverty?" *The New Media Journal*, August 23, 2007. Copyright © JR Dieckmann. Reproduced by permission of the author.

As you read, consider the following questions:

1. What are some of the consequences of the U.S. government providing aid to third world countries?

2. According to the author, all foreign aid must be replaced with what kind of programs?

3. How long does the author believe it will take the U.S. government to phase out providing aid to third world countries?

We have all seen close-up how welfare handouts from the U.S. Treasury maintain a poverty level income for those who refuse to—or are unable to—work. The same concept applies to the "victims" of U.S. foreign aid.

America Is a Self-Made Country

First, there is something that we need to understand about our own country. The United States of America is not the typical country of the world. It is the exception. The standard of living and prosperity that we tend to take for granted is far superior to the average nation on Earth. That didn't happen by accident; there are reasons for it.

One reason is that Americans fought for our freedom and liberty—and some still do—while others prefer peace at any price. The freedom and liberty that our ancestors fought for is what opened the door for American creativity, ingenuity, and consequent prosperity. We weren't born wealthy, we earned it.

No one gave early Americans foreign aid to pay their way. We did it all on our own. We worked and fought for every dollar we earned without the restrictions of overbearing, big government. As a result, we created our own prosperity, culture, and standard of living. We have continued to work hard to improve that standard ever since. Simply put, we have the standard of living that we enjoy because that is who we are.

Because we now live in a generation that just accepts the American standard of living as expected, we forget what it took to bring us to this point. We tend to think that everyone should live the way we do in America, and when we look at third world countries we feel it's our responsibility to help them out of their own poverty. We tend to see them as disadvantaged, but that is only from our point of view.

What we fail to understand is that the way of life in third world countries is just as normal for them as our way of life is normal for us. Liberal "do-gooders" and charity organizations will find the most depressed areas in the world to display in the media, in order to provoke our "feelings" and try to persuade us to give money to their cause. When we do give, some of that money actually does go to people in third world countries to help provide food, medicine, and clothing. Much of it does not. It stays in the pockets of organizations and tyrannical dictators.

This isn't very different from advertising techniques that use the "worst case" examples to sell their products and services. There is nothing intrinsically wrong with that. As long as people are given the choice of contributing money to them or not, then there is no harm done. As it turns out, Americans are the most generous people in the world.

Indebting Foreign Lands

But then our politicians decide that they should show that they also care and mandate our taxpayers' money to foreign charity. Don't expect the members of Congress to give their own money to help people in these third world countries. It's much easier for them simply to confiscate our money to provide foreign aid while ignoring the Constitution, which never authorized them to do so.

There is nothing that Congress likes to do more than to spend money that doesn't belong to them. They don't even wait to see if there is any money left in the budget to spend on nonessential earmarks. The personal pork comes first; then they find legislation to attach it to. They spend billions of dol-

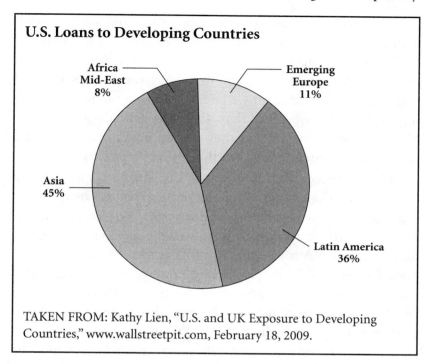

U.S. Loans to Developing Countries

Africa Mid-East 8%

Emerging Europe 11%

Asia 45%

Latin America 36%

TAKEN FROM: Kathy Lien, "U.S. and UK Exposure to Developing Countries," www.wallstreetpit.com, February 18, 2009.

lars of our money on things that we would never approve of and they get it passed through Congress simply because it has been attached to some essential legislation. It's time for Congress to put a stop to this corrupt and unethical practice.

So what happens when the United States Congress gives away money to third world countries? It's pretty much the same thing that happens here when credit card and finance companies promote the borrowing of money and encourage people to live beyond their means. We are now starting to see the consequences of that with the current mortgage company crunch and people losing their homes—homes that they never should have bought in the first place because they couldn't afford them. And to top it off, now some people are calling for a taxpayer bailout so that we all can pay for the mistakes of others and assure them that they can continue to live beyond their means.

That takes us back to foreign aid where the same thing is happening. We have attempted to artificially raise the standard of living for people in poverty-ridden countries above what would be normal for that country. They come to depend on that aid just like those on welfare and use it to enjoy a slightly higher standard of living than they can actually afford. This higher standard means that they can afford to live longer and have more children, adding to the country's population.

The resources of any country can support only just so much population. When the population expands beyond what the national resources can support, you have chaos, unrest and wars. This is our gift to third world countries. Without it, nature would control population to a level a country can support. Foreign aid is simply adding to an already overcrowded world population and providing nothing of value in return. Most countries receiving U.S. foreign aid oppose us in world politics and foreign policy; many ally with our enemies.

I know this may sound harsh, but without foreign aid, the population of third world countries would be limited to what those countries can support. Yes, more would die and fewer would be born, but that's the way it should be. It's like water seeking its own level when two containers are connected together. One container holds the population; the other contains the national resources. They tend to balance.

U.S. foreign aid has upset that balance in third world countries, and now we are committed to continuously adding more water to the resource container. In the end, there is no improvement in third world living conditions. The population is merely expanded, adding to the problem. The poverty continues just as it has been, only more people are now living with it.

Taking Responsibility

It's the same thing that is happening in the American ghetto. Government cannot end poverty. It is up to the people living with it to get off their asses and make a better life for themselves. That is the only way their accomplishments will be worth anything to them. If they refuse to make the effort, then they are not only useless to society, but a burden on it. We must stop coddling these useless wastes of protoplasm and calling them "victims." They are victims only of themselves and that is—and always has been—their own choice. You have the right to screw up your life in America. You do not have the right to hold the taxpayers responsible for it.

The solution lies in the old adage: "A Democrat will give a man a fish. A Republican will teach the man how to fish." All foreign aid must stop and be replaced with educating people of the world in how to improve their own lives. We can show them the path to success, but we cannot do it for them.

But that won't be easy. It's going to take a great deal more than just education. It's going to take major changes in society and government of these countries to make it happen. We can hold America up as an example and show them how free enterprise and profit motivation can create wonders. We can show them how a free people, unrestricted by excessive government oppression, will allow the human spirit to flourish and create. But they must develop a system and a government that will support it, not destroy it.

It's going to take something like a 100-year program to transition a country from a poverty state to a prosperous state. We can only suggest such a program, and it will be up to the people of those countries to enact it. They will have to start looking toward the future of their country and must want to make the changes for the sake of their children and their children's children.

We can encourage them to begin by putting them on notice that foreign aid from America will start to decline year by year, and that it's going to be up to them to make the necessary changes to support themselves without our help in the end. If they choose not to make those changes, then pull the plug on foreign aid and let their country's population take its natural course and reduce itself through attrition.

We have to consider also that some nations would rather not develop as America has. Some may prefer the simple and uncomplicated life. We must respect that choice to allow them to live the way they want to, as long as they can do it without U.S. foreign aid. Our federal government has—and wrongly in my opinion—imposed requirements on local school districts in order to have access to federal funds. This same requirement should apply to countries receiving foreign aid in America's "no country left behind" program. Otherwise, we are just throwing away good money after bad.

Respect the Development Patterns of Other Nations

People who say that America should share our wealth with other nations are usually not the people who have created the wealth. They are the global socialists who want to redistribute American wealth created and owned by people other than themselves. They desire a global, level playing field, which will make it much easier for world domination by global socialists. Their global warming fraud represents their current attempt to do just that. Each country needs to grow and develop in its own way. They cannot be pushed or helped out of poverty with handouts, if poverty—in the view of Americans—is the standard for their country.

America cannot continue to carry the whole world on its back. There are too many countries in the world where people just want to earn enough money to leave and come to America instead of helping their own country out of poverty. This too needs to stop. We have enough people in the U.S. We don't need any more.

It's time to curtail immigration into our country altogether, at least for a limited time. Since we can't seem to control our own immigration and population, we need to close our borders until we can.

Above all, our politicians and our president need to consider the needs of America first before we try to play the role of provider to other countries. We give away money to foreign powers who use it to buy weapons to kill Americans. We allow foreign students and others to enter our country, even from the Middle East who may very well end up as domestic terrorists. Politicians and our president have put our country in grave danger with their immigration policies and foreign aid when their first priority should be the welfare and security of American citizens. Until U.S. immigration and foreign policy are radically changed, we will not see safety and security in America, nor will we be able to maintain our prosperity for very much longer.

Periodical Bibliography

The following articles have been selected to supplement the diverse views presented in this chapter.

Patrick J. Buchanan	"Depression Factory," *American Conservative*, April 29, 2009.
Dennis Cauchon	"States and Cities Borrow Big," *USA Today*, May 4, 2009.
Consumer Reports	"Now Your Credit Is Bailing Out Banks," May 2009.
Mark Gongloff	"Government Holds Strings to Markets," *The Wall Street Journal*, May 11, 2009.
William P. Hoar	"Printing and Spending Our Way to Prosperity," *New American*, April 27, 2009.
Kimberly Lankford	"Stimulus Straight Talk," *Kiplinger's Personal Finance*, June 2009.
The New York Times Magazine	"Diminished Returns," May 31, 2009.
Paul Ormerod	"Don't Panic," *New Statesman*, May 11, 2009.
Nomi Prins	"Risk Is Best Managed from the Bottom Up," *American Prospect*, May 2009.
Charles Scaliger	"Creating 'Wealth,'" *New American*, April 13, 2009.
John Sfakianakis	"Lessons Learned," *Time Atlantic*, May 25, 2009.
David Streitfeld	"An Inquiry into Firms That Offer to Cut Debt," *The New York Times*, May 8, 2009.

OPPOSING
VIEWPOINTS®
SERIES

CHAPTER 4

How Can Debt Problems Be Solved?

Chapter Preface

According to a February 2009 Federal Reserve Report, American consumer revolving debt, a category made up almost entirely of credit cards, grew to $961.3 billion. Add in the climbing unemployment rate, the mortgage bust, and the spike in bankruptcy filings, and it is no wonder that consumers are grasping at any debt solution that might come their way. As evidence of this growing crisis, debt consolidation companies, also known as credit counseling agencies, have become big business in the United States, pocketing $7 billion annually, estimates MSN Money. Unfortunately, not all of these companies are out to help consumers, and recent reports have revealed that some deliberately exploit clients seeking help for their financial problems.

The theory behind credit counseling is a good one. Consumers struggling to pay off their debts work with an agency to create a financial plan that often involves lenders cutting interest rates or reducing balances. In turn, clients in crisis can then re-pay their debts while avoiding bankruptcy. Although some lenders view enrollment in credit counseling as negative, far more institutions view bankruptcy as liability. In fact, some companies are likely to look favorably upon customers who seek credit repayment through a counseling firm. In a statement made to MSN Money, Citibank spokeswoman Maria Mendler notes, "We always viewed that as a positive. We've seen that for people who enter these programs, there's a significantly lower rate of default." In other words, for some consumers who are deep in debt, credit counseling might help them pay off their loans and improve their standing with borrowers.

Unfortunately, not all credit counselors are helpful. Some take advantage of consumers during their most difficult time by charging them exorbitant processing fees and making them promises that they cannot keep. "Credit Counseling in Crisis," a 2003 report produced by the National Consumer Law Center (NCLC) and Consumer Federation of America (CFA), reveals that "unlike the previous generation of mostly creditor-funded counseling services, these new agencies often harm debtors with improper advice, deceptive practices, excessive fees, and abuse of their nonprofit status." Deanne Loonin, staff attorney for the NCLC, says, "Aggressive firms masquerading as 'nonprofit organizations' are gouging consumers. Deceptive practices and outright scams are on the rise. More consumers are getting bad advice and access to fewer real counseling options." Even though some consumers are trying to dig their way out of debt, a growing number of fraudulent credit counselors are pushing them closer to bankruptcy.

Given the credit crisis, finding a solution to debt repayment is a bigger challenge than ever before. But as the authors in this chapter debate, determining the best plan of action is difficult. For some, credit counseling might be the answer, but the increasing number of fraudulent agencies have caused many consumers to be wary of this kind of support.

"There are ways of navigating the rough waters of bankruptcy that make it easier to emerge on the other side, better positioned to make a fresh start."

Declaring Bankruptcy Can Help Families Start Over

Laura Cohn

Laura Cohn is a regular contributor to Kiplinger's Personal Finance. *In the following viewpoint, she argues that although bankruptcy can make credit scores plummet, the overall advantages of filing can help filers begin again. Because the federal government requires filers to seek credit counseling beforehand and to take personal finance classes afterward, bankruptcy can be the best solution for struggling consumers who want the opportunity to rebuild their lives.*

As you read, consider the following questions:

1. What is the means test?

2. What is an upside-down mortgage?

3. According to estimates, how many points does filing bankruptcy take off of the average credit score?

Stephanie Monson was horrified when she learned that her husband had racked up more than $45,000 in credit card bills. The debt forced Monson to file for personal bankruptcy—and led to the couple's divorce.

With the help of an attorney, Monson filed for Chapter 7, a process that wipes the debt slate clean but also requires the liquidation of major assets. In the end, Monson's massive mound of credit card debt was forgiven. And because she wasn't behind on her mortgage payments, her lawyer worked out a payment plan with her lender that allowed her to keep her home.

Getting out from under all that debt was a relief, but two years later the consequences continue to resonate. "My sterling credit rating went down the drain," says Monson, a mother of three who is an academic adviser at the College of St. Scholastica, in Duluth, Minn.

The experience made Monson reassess her personal finances in a way she never thought she'd have to. She recently started using budgeting software to track her spending and get a feel for where her money is going. She now has only one credit card, which she pays off every month. Monson says she's taken all these steps because "I need to be an example for the kids."

As more people start to veer off financial course, Monson presents a reassuring example of how to slowly and deliberately rebuilt a fiscal foundation after a financial crisis.

Spreading Pain

Falling home prices, a swooning stock market and sky-high levels of consumer debt have left many Americans little choice but to consider personal bankruptcy. Filings rose more than 30% last year [2008] compared with 2007, to 1.1 million, according to the American Bankruptcy Institute [ABI], a research and education organization. Filings are likely to increase by another 35% in 2009, according to an ABI poll.

The pain is spreading: In the past, personal bankruptcy was mainly the province of lower-income families. Now credit counselors and bankruptcy lawyers report that more and more upper-income households are being pushed to the brink by one or more financial crises—unaffordable home payments, job loss, divorce or a major illness that insurance doesn't cover. Laura Margulies, a consumer-bankruptcy attorney in Rockville, Md., says that until recently she was dealing with construction and real estate workers who had fallen on hard times. Now she is receiving inquiries about filing from people in all walks of life.

As a rule, personal bankruptcy should be a last resort. But as Monson discovered, there are ways of navigating the rough waters of bankruptcy that make it easier to emerge on the other side, better positioned to make a fresh start.

Tougher Standards

If you're considering bankruptcy, the first thing to do is hire a lawyer. The Bankruptcy Abuse Prevention and Consumer Protection Act of 2005 made filing far more complex, so you should find an attorney who specializes in consumer bankruptcies. Under the new law, passed after heavy lobbying by credit card companies and other lenders, you'll have a tougher time proving that your financial straits are truly dire. To qualify, you have to provide more paperwork and meet stricter standards.

As a consumer, the two main types of bankruptcy available to you are Chapter 7 and Chapter 13. (If you owe more than $1.3 million, you can enter into Chapter 11.)

By far the most common form for individuals is Chapter 7, which essentially amounts to a liquidation. If you've lost your job, are overwhelmed with debt and earn less than the median income, you most likely will file for this type of bankruptcy. Your assets—possibly including your house—are sold and the proceeds are divided among your creditors.

Chapter 7 gives you a clean slate because all IOUs—with the exception of taxes, child support and student loans—are discharged. To qualify, you must undergo a "means test"; you can file if you earn less than the median income for a family of similar size in your state. In Maryland for instance, you must earn less than $53,489 as an individual or less than $71,000 as a two-person family. The U.S. Census Bureau tracks the median family income on a state-by-state basis.

If you are drowning in debt but have a job, you may qualify for Chapter 13. Those who file for this type of bankruptcy typically earn more than the median family income. You have to have discretionary income, which can include income from a job, self-employment or a family member who agrees to help out.

Consumers facing foreclosure who want to keep their home are the largest group of Chapter 13 filers. Chapter 13 may also work for you if you owe back taxes, child support or student loans, which wouldn't be eliminated by a Chapter 7 filing. Under Chapter 13, your attorney proposes a three- to five-year repayment plan to the court that outlines who gets paid each month.

If you qualify for both Chapter 7 and Chapter 13, your financial priorities will help determine which type you should file. One of the key factors in the decision is whether you want to keep your home. With so many homeowners "upside down" on their mortgage—meaning they owe more than their house is worth—some want to start fresh, even with the hit to their credit score. In that case, Chapter 7 would be the more attractive option.

Before you file for bankruptcy, you must see a counselor at a credit-counseling agency that has been approved by the U.S. Department of Justice. Some agencies charge for the initial session, but they'll waive the fee if you ask for an exemption prior to the session.

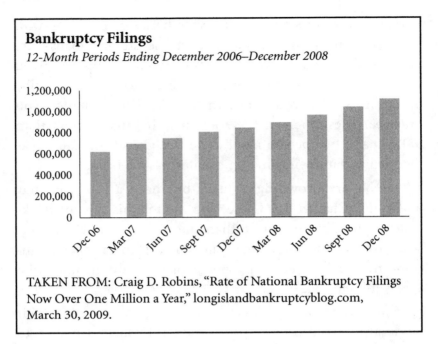

Bankruptcy Filings

12-Month Periods Ending December 2006–December 2008

TAKEN FROM: Craig D. Robins, "Rate of National Bankruptcy Filings Now Over One Million a Year," longislandbankruptcyblog.com, March 30, 2009.

Then after you file for bankruptcy, you must complete a debtor-education course intended to teach you how to budget your money and use credit carefully. The debtor-education provider, who will charge a fee between $50 and $100, must also be approved by the Justice Department. You can find a state-by-state list of qualified credit counselors and debtor-education agencies at the Justice Department's Web site.

Should You Do It?

Perhaps the most far-reaching consequence of filing for bankruptcy is the impact on your credit. A bankruptcy filing stays on your credit record for seven to ten years, says Steven Katz, director of consumer education at TrueCredit.com, the consumer branch of the credit bureau TransUnion. While the impact on your credit score depends on your individual situation, some bankruptcy lawyers say it could take a hit of 100 points. That's why the decision to file is not one that you should take lightly.

In fact, if you're starting to feel overwhelmed with debt, it's a good idea to seek credit counseling before payments get out of control. "If you catch things early enough, you may not have to file for bankruptcy," says Bruce McClary, media relations coordinator and a certified counselor for ClearPoint Financial Solutions, in Richmond, Va. You could also tap the free information and budgeting tips on the Web site of the American Financial Services Association, the trade group for the consumer credit industry.

The Federal Trade Commission says the number of individuals approaching credit counselors has jumped by more than one-third recently. In some cases, your credit counselor can work out a repayment plan with your creditors. Your lawyer may also be able to negotiate a deal with lenders.

In the end, if there is no other way out, be sure you don't get sucked into a credit-counseling scam. Such schemes are becoming more common in the down economy.

> "*[Bankruptcy] is the most painful process, something that is irrevocably life-changing and should surely only ever be seen as the very last resort.*"

Declaring Bankruptcy Can Destroy Families

Alison Smith-Squire

Alison Smith-Squire is a writer based in the United Kingdom. Her work has appeared in The Daily Mail, The Mirror, The Sun, *and* The Sunday Mirror. *In the following viewpoint, she tells the story of Gabrielle Sneddon-Pike, whose family deteriorated after filing bankruptcy. A bad business deal led to the dissolution of her family's wealth and eventually her marriage. Contrary to common belief, Sneddon-Pike found that bankruptcy is not an easy way out of debt, but one of the most difficult crises that any marriage can face.*

As you read, consider the following questions:

1. During the second quarter of 2006, how many people went bankrupt in England and Wales?

2. How did Sneddon-Pike's family go bankrupt?

3. When did Sneddon-Pike realize that her marriage was over?

Bankruptcy affects thousands of people every year in the UK [United Kingdom].

New figures show that a record 26,000 people—almost one every minute of every working day—were made bankrupt in England and Wales during the second quarter of this year [2006]. Experts now predict personal insolvencies will exceed 100,000 by the end of the year.

Gabrielle Sneddon-Pike, 45, lost her country house and her 20-year marriage after her husband Paul, 52, was made bankrupt. Here, Gabrielle, from Hampshire, who has an 18-year-old daughter, Lulu, talks about the family's anguish:

Until my husband Paul was made bankrupt, money problems were something that happened to other people. In fact, I'm sure to everyone who knew us we seemed to have a gilded life.

We lived in a large five-bedroom country house with three acres and had a Range Rover, a BMW and a sporty Golf in the garages. We enjoyed fantastic holidays abroad with our daughter, Lulu. Paul's parents lived in a cottage on the grounds and we kept a pony and a horse in stables just down the road.

I also had a career that I loved. As a magazine correspondent interviewing people in the music business, I often travelled abroad. We employed nannies and, later, a housekeeper to keep things ticking over while I was away.

Paul and I met through work. I was a writer and he was a marketing consultant. We married in April 1982 and, shortly afterwards, Paul started up his own marketing business.

His business went from strength to strength, and before long we were able to afford to move from our town house in Richmond, Surrey, to our dream home in the country.

We both worked incredibly hard, and although we never considered ourselves super-rich, we enjoyed all the trappings of a luxury lifestyle. We shared a love of good restaurants, horse-riding, the outdoors, water sports and travelling.

Best of all, though, Paul was everything I'd ever wanted in a husband: he was kind, funny, a marvellous dad and my best friend.

The Bottom Fell Out

But, in the spring of 1992, our lives were turned upside down. I came home from work one day to find the house unusually quiet. Paul was home, but instead of greeting me as usual, he was slumped in a chair in the living room. As soon as he looked up at me, his face white and ashen, I knew that something was wrong.

'Something terrible has happened,' he said. 'I may be made bankrupt.' I can still remember the shock I felt—I'd had absolutely no idea.

Paul went on to explain that a business deal had gone dreadfully wrong. It was complex what had happened, but he explained the company had lost a great deal of money.

It may sound unbelievable, but it was a total and utter shock. I could hardly take in what he was saying. Paul was always busy, I was busy, and we concentrated on our own jobs. We never had any reason to discuss each other's business.

There had been no lead-up, no telltale signs that this was coming. And, from Paul's face I could tell that he, too, was in total disbelief.

Though we did not know it at the time, it was to be the beginning of a ten-year nightmare that would tear our lives apart.

Over the next few weeks, I consoled myself that the worst might not happen. Paul worked day and night to try to stave off the bankruptcy—but it was to no avail. Within months he lost the company he'd so lovingly built up and was officially declared bankrupt.

Losing It All

By going bankrupt, people are freed of their debts but lose all control over their own finances. To repay creditors, all of their bank accounts can be emptied and their assets sold.

We were totally unprepared. I had no idea what happens during a bankruptcy, but it seemed as if, overnight, our lives changed completely.

From being a company director whose days were full of phone calls, conferences and lunches, Paul was suddenly at home all day, lonely and rudderless. Unlike someone else who's lost their job, there was no redundancy cheque [payments received when a job is lost due to layoff] to fall back on. Indeed, as a bankrupt, he was no longer allowed even to have a bank account.

A few weeks later, I came home to find all three of our cars had gone. They were bought on finance and had been repossessed. It was so shaming. It seemed we were losing everything that had given us the status we cherished.

I worked every spare hour to earn extra money to keep us afloat. Suddenly being without my husband's substantial five-figure salary was a devastating shock.

The bills came in as usual; the weekly shopping had to be bought. My salary simply couldn't stretch to cover everything.

So we did what most people do when they don't have enough money to live on: we remortgaged our house.

Major Lifestyle Changes

At first, with the money from the house, life didn't seem too bad. But we soon began eating into the capital from the new mortgage.

We cut back drastically on our lifestyle and used credit cards to fund household bills. We let the housekeeper go and stopped going out to restaurants and on holidays.

I used to shop in designer boutiques but now I browsed second-hand shops, saving all the money I could for our daughter's essentials, such as school shoes and uniform.

I sold off many of my designer clothes and Paul didn't buy any new clothes at all. It was as though we had regressed financially by about 15 years.

Living in the country had seemed so idyllic, but now it became a problem. We were in the middle of nowhere, with little public transport, and life was impossible without our own car.

We bought a second-hand Fiesta, but having to share the one car meant giving each another lifts and added to the strain.

Gradually, our debts began mounting. Once, opening the mail had been an enjoyable breakfast ritual, but now the sound of the post on the mat made my heart thud with worry. I dreaded the phone ringing, too, in case it was a demand for money.

Neither Paul nor I could sleep properly. And when I did sleep, I'd wake up in the morning feeling sick and worn out. Some days I could not even eat—I just lost my appetite. On my worst days, I'd lock myself in the bathroom and sob for hours.

Paul spent hours poring over his old company books. He became almost obsessed with it, trying to work out where the business had gone wrong and seeing if there was any way out.

He looked for other marketing work, but the bankruptcy always got in the way. As soon as people found out, they didn't want to know. It restricted what he did and he couldn't start another business or get credit.

Our relationship began to suffer, too. I'd vowed to stand by Paul and was sure we could get through this difficult time and emerge a stronger couple—but although we tried to communicate, it was always about money and the misery we found ourselves in.

Isolated

We would sit and have serious talks for hours, going round and round the same old issues but not making any headway. We felt so isolated.

It seemed as if there was no way out and no one who could help us. Even my beautiful home—once a sanctuary— now seemed to be my enemy. Because it was such a big place, it ate money. Yet the thought of letting it go was unbearable.

It is a very humbling thing to admit that as a couple you have failed somehow and are in financial meltdown. I couldn't tell my family what we were going through. We didn't even tell Paul's parents, who lived in a cottage within our grounds.

I've no doubt that there are thousands of middle-class families like us who simply cannot bring themselves to tell even those closest to them. Bankruptcy is such a stigma to carry.

So to the world I just had to put on a brave face. I'd have our daughter's friends over to play as usual and pick her up from school. At work, I never told a soul about my problems at home.

But the strain of keeping up the pretence that everything was fine was enormous. I felt as if I could never be happy. Our financial situation was always there, nagging away at the back of my mind.

At least no one considered it odd that Paul wasn't going to work any more. He'd always had an office at home, so people just assumed he was working from there.

In any case, Paul couldn't bring himself to tell anyone what was going on. I think he was just too embarrassed. He'd always been so outgoing and chatty, but now he became very quiet, locked in his own private world.

We tried to keep life as normal as possible, though, and still shared a bed. We still loved one another and we told our-selves that we would get through it together. We took each day as it came. Money was obviously tight and every day meant a financial juggle, but we lived like paupers and tried to eke out my salary to cover the bare essentials.

After five years of living like this, though, we began drifting apart. At this time, my work was my salvation and I threw myself into it. In effect, Paul and I swapped roles, with me becoming the main breadwinner and Paul looking after our daughter. He was very supportive and tried to pull his weight.

Then, just before Christmas 2000, we had the letter we'd dreaded. With our mortgage in arrears, the bank had written to say a repossession order had been put on the house.

Tears rolled down my cheeks as I read that letter—yet I knew the house had become a millstone around our necks. We'd already put the house on the market. We knew it had to go.

That Christmas was terrible. We had the pressure of keeping up the appearances of normality for mine and Paul's parents, despite knowing we had to cut back on spending on presents and celebrations. My mother had been ill with cancer and I knew it would break her heart to know what was going on.

Hardly Speaking

Meanwhile, the atmosphere in the house was incredibly tense. Paul and I were hardly speaking to one another. I didn't hate him—we just couldn't talk to each other.

Then, at the start of the New Year, came an eviction order. Thankfully, days before the repossession order was to be executed we exchanged contracts. We'd sold the house for over £500,000. We'd both hoped that after paying back the mortgage and other debts, such as unpaid bills and credit cards, there might be a tiny bit left. But although we emerged debt-free, there was hardly a penny left from the sale.

And by then I knew our marriage was over. Our money worries had simply driven us apart. We didn't even argue—

Bankruptcy Should Only Be Used as a Last Resort

Compelling as it may sound, bankruptcy has a lingering and far-reaching impact that touches every aspect of life. Bankruptcy ruins credit, makes it difficult, if not impossible, to keep bank accounts and credit cards, can take some valued, and valuable, possessions, and makes it difficult to get on with necessities of life such as buying or renting a home or car, getting insurance and finding a job.

In fact, most financial advisors look at bankruptcy as a desperate last resort, when budgeting, credit counseling and other efforts to get out of debt have failed, and then only with the advice and guidance of an experienced bankruptcy attorney.

"When, Why, and Why Not, Should You Consider Bankruptcy?" April 2009. http://bankruptcy-law.freeadvice.com.

there was just a tense silence between us. All the joy had gone out of our relationship. It was simply unsalvageable and I filed for divorce.

We both managed to find separate properties to rent. Sorting through the furniture and detritus of our life together, deciding who should have what, was simply the saddest thing.

By now Lulu was 13 and she knew we were separating, but I reassured her she would still see as much of her dad as she wanted. I kept positive. Eventually, I managed to save a small deposit and buy a modest house to share with my daughter.

Lulu was upset but really it came as a relief to her because we'd been living under terrible pressure.

I missed my big old house terribly—especially the fantastic kitchen and the wonderful fireplaces—but it was also a relief that the whole nightmare was finally over.

After the End

Five years on, I have emerged stronger and wiser. I realise I don't need material possessions or to go to posh restaurants to be happy. I enjoy myself now by simple means—cooking at home, going for walks and meeting friends.

I made a decision to move forward and not let what happened ruin the rest of my life. Instead, I counted my blessings: my job and my daughter.

Paul and I have kept in regular contact. He's still a wonderful father and our daughter sees him regularly.

I don't hate him—he was a victim of circumstances. Looking back, his only fault was perhaps he was simply too nice and too trusting. I honestly think if this hadn't happened we would still be happily married now.

I'm not bitter, but I haven't met anyone else—certainly no one I would want to have a relationship with. And the spectre of bankruptcy still haunts me. Ten years of suffering, of watching every penny, of continually having to think about how much money you're spending, have taken their toll.

Even today, money problems seem a taboo subject. It's not something I bring up in casual conversation. I wish I had known more about my husband's business, and a shiver still runs through me whenever I read about households with money problems.

Most of all, I find it incredible that some people today view bankruptcy as an easy way out of financial trouble. It is the most painful process, something that is irrevocably life-changing and should surely only ever be seen as the very last resort.

> "I really think that the Army route is for me for so many reasons besides financially."

Joining the Military Is an Effective Way to Pay Off Student Loans

Janet Kidd Stewart

Janet Kidd Stewart is a columnist for the Chicago Tribune *from which the following viewpoint is excerpted. She tells the story of Jim Burzynski, a college student who will be in deep debt by the time he graduates. He has many options for his future, but after meeting with a financial counselor, he has decided to join the U.S. military. By doing so, Burzynski will earn a salary and be able to pay off his debts through the military's loan forgiveness program.*

As you read, consider the following questions:

1. How much will Burzynski owe in student loans by the time he graduates from college?

2. In addition to joining the Army, what are some other options that Burzynski considered?

3. In terms of net worth, why is the Army the best choice for Burzynski?

Jim Burzynski has a bright future, but it has cost him.

The 24-year-old will graduate in March [2007] with a degree in one of today's most in-demand careers—pharmacy—where he could command $100,000 or more in starting salary.

But getting there hasn't been easy. On his own since he turned 18, Burzynski knew he needed a solid education to support himself, so he took on loads of student loans and odd jobs to finance a spot at Midwestern University College of Pharmacy in Downers Grove [Illinois].

He's already tallied up $119,000 in student loans, and by the time he graduates, he expects he'll owe about $150,000.

And he's not even sure he wants one of those six-figure starting salaries. Those jobs are typically in the retail pharmacy field, but Burzynski has other ideas: He's considering joining the military, and yearns to work in an academic environment, possibly even doing a pharmacy residency at a teaching hospital, which would pay far less, about $40,000 annually for two to three years.

Tack on his desire to retire at 50 to a second career as a business owner, and it appears Burzynski's dreams are out of reach.

"It's pretty scary" to contemplate the size of his student loan debt, let alone the steps needed to reach early retirement, he said.

But like other debt-laden twentysomethings just starting out, Burzynski has a lot of time on his side to make his financial goals work out, said Julie Schatz, a financial planner with Investor's Capital Management in Menlo Park, Calif.

"The [debt] number sounds daunting, but you are fortunate to have strong earning power, and starting the financial planning process at your age is a huge boon," Schatz said.

"Making concrete plans and having specific goals in your head will make it more likely you'll get where you want to be."

Developing a Strategy

To get Burzynski started out on the right financial foot after graduation, he first needs to decide on a strategy for tackling those student loans. Schatz estimated his payments will come to about $970 a month.

He's been contemplating those different post-graduation options. First is taking the highest paying retail pharmacy job he can find, hopefully snagging a salary high enough that he'll stand a chance at paying back the loans.

He's also thought about the residency option, but Schatz said that option really isn't economically feasible.

The military option has appeal, in part because of loan forgiveness programs in exchange for a number of years of service.

Concerns about his safety aside, Schatz ran the numbers to see which strategy—the Army or the retail pharmacy job—made the most sense.

The Army would pay less than half of what a private-sector job would—about $40,000 a year—but the loan forgiveness of up to about $122,000 over about four years, plus room and board allowances and a lighter tax load, would offset the lower pay, the adviser said.

By the end of 2011, under the Army plan and following some savings guidelines, his liquid assets would be $4,000, and total assets (including investments) would be about $32,000. By contrast, with a private job, he would have $18,000 in liquid savings and total assets of $84,000.

So why is the Army route better? After the loan forgiveness program, he would have a negative net worth in four years of $35,396. If he had to pay off his loans alone with the higher-paying job, his net worth in 2011 would be a negative $66,591, Schatz projects.

"Trevor, it's some gentlemen to see you about your student loan." Cartoon by Kes. www.CartoonStock.com

"Jim's net worth, while still negative after four years, is higher with the Army," she said. Military service would mean lower federal taxes because of the lower income, no state taxes because of his exemption and lower expenses because of food and shelter allowances.

Learning Life Skills

And then there are the intangibles. Burzynski thinks Army training will let him see the world and teach him invaluable life skills that he'll be able to parlay into his future career endeavors.

By contrast, a higher-paying retail pharmacy job might seem rote and limiting after a couple of years, he worries.

Even after the career decision is made, Burzynski needs to do some other things to get his adult financial life started, Schatz said.

He's already doing a pretty good job of tracking monthly expenses and has searched out online checking and savings accounts paying the most competitive interest rates.

But when income starts flowing after graduation, he needs to build an emergency fund of $15,000, Schatz said. To do that, he'll need to trim his college-days spending on going to restaurants, sporting events and clubs. He's currently dropping about $1,000 a month on restaurants and entertainment, and Schatz would like to see him cut that by $300.

With more than $2,000 in credit card debt, he should try to lower the interest payments on his two credit cards (now 20 percent and 30 percent) by contacting the card companies or shopping around for low-interest balance-transfer offers.

He should sign up for the federal Thrift Savings Plan if he joins the Army (or for an employer's 401(k) plan), but only contribute $2,000 with the government plan or $5,000 with a private employer plan.

Why?

With the Army, he will be in the 15 percent federal tax bracket, likely a lower bracket than where he'll be at retirement, when he'll have to pay the income tax on that money at withdrawal.

Even with a private employer, he'll be better off plowing as much as possible into a Roth individual retirement account—in which later withdrawals are tax-free—while his income still allows it, she said.

Contributing to a 401(k) can also keep his income from hitting Roth eligibility limits, which has a phase-out range for single filers is $99,000 to $114,000 in modified adjusted gross income for 2007.

Saving for the Future

Finally, once he's working, he'll need to start saving in a taxable savings account. "The after-tax account is very important for future purchases like a condo and a car," Schatz said. "If you truly want to retire early, you'll have to have money in a taxable account that you can pull from until you're eligible to withdraw from retirement accounts."

Despite the significant debt that will follow Burzynski through at least the next several years, Schatz said he has a good chance at succeeding financially because of his early interest in planning for the future and his past record of getting himself to this point.

"This is great," Burzynski said after completing the Money Makeover process. "I finally have a good picture of what is going to happen financially for me once I am done.

"As to which path I will go, I really think that the Army route is for me for so many reasons besides financially. I really believe it will make me a better, stronger person and there is a possibility of completing a residency with the Army, which would be the best-paying residency in the country because of the loan forgiveness.

"My only stumbling block with this route is my need to get back in shape."

> "The anger is now being organized into a drive to keep military recruiters off the university campus and out of the students' private communications."

Military Recruiters Use Loan Forgiveness to Target Students

Ron Jacobs

Ron Jacobs is the author of The Way the Wind Blew: A History of the Weather Underground, *which chronicles the beginnings of a radical student organization that was formed in the 1960s. In the following viewpoint, he argues that joining the military is most likely not the best way to pay off student loan debts. In fact, the military's heavy recruitment strategies aimed at college students continue to cause controversy. In response, student organizations across the country are protesting their presence on college campuses.*

As you read, consider the following questions:

1. What is the Solomon Amendment?

2. How many high schools across the country give the AS-VAB test?

3. Why did the federal appeals court agree that universities can ban military recruiters from visiting their campuses?

Recently, most students at the University of Vermont (UVM) in Burlington received an e-mail with the heading ARMY PAYS OFF STUDENT LOANS in their university e-mail box. The general message of the mass mailing was that if a student was nearing graduation and wondering how they were going to pay off the massive debt today's US college students incur, they should join the army. In essence, this e-mail was a college student's version of the poverty draft that entraps so many working class and poor young people into enlisting in the service. The sender was a military recruiter working out of the US Army recruitment office in the Burlington suburb of Williston. Given that the university has a very clear policy forbidding these types of solicitations on their e-mail servers one wonders how the recruiting office was able to obtain the address list. The university administration has been reticent when asked this question by various faculty, students, and parents. It is fair to assume, however, that the e-mail list was released to the recruiter under the compliance sections of the so-called Solomon Amendment. For those unfamiliar with this legislation, it essentially forbids Department of Defense (DOD) funding of schools unless those schools provide military representatives access to their students for recruiting purposes. It is this same law that enables military recruiters to set up shop in high schools across the US and to call students at their homes attempting to entice them into joining the military.

At UVM, this e-mail was met with anger and questions, and probably even a few inquiries. The anger is now being organized into a drive to keep military recruiters off the university campus and out of the students' private communications. There is a petition campaign underway that demands that no recruiters for the regular military or the Vermont National

Does the GI Bill Still Pay?

Matthew Schelberg enlisted in the Marine Corps Reserves in 2001 and took part in the invasion of Iraq two years later. He spent six months south of Baghdad and returned for a second tour in Haditha that ended earlier this year [2007]. Like his grandfather, Schelberg went from an overseas deployment to a college classroom. But as he studies at Bucknell University, the debt piles up. Schelberg's GI Bill, a scaled-down version of the original, pays less than one tenth of his university and housing fees, which come to $46,000 a year. By graduation, he expects to have taken out $60,000 in student loans.

Dan Ephron, "A Learning Disability,"
Newsweek, *November 26, 2007.*

Guard be allowed to recruit on campus. Despite this, recruiters do show up unannounced on campus. One assumes that their strategy is designed to prevent student organizers from organizing protests against the recruiters' presence. In addition, there is organizing underway to organize some kind of response to the military and Guard's presence at the University's Spring Career Day on March 8th [2005]. (This career day is also the host to recruiters from various corporations from the war industry—General Dynamics foremost among them). Here in Vermont, the Guard recruitment hits close to home, since the state ranks near the top in the number of deaths per capita in Iraq. The likelihood of the university denying these recruiters access is slim, especially in light of the mass e-mail, yet the students involved continue on undaunted. If the petition campaign fails to produce the results they desire, there will likely be some kind of protest.

Other Campus Protests

Other college campuses have already experienced such protests. On January 20, 2005, several hundred students at Seattle Central Community College chased army recruiters from their spot in the student center. On February 23, campus police arrested a woman student during a picket in front of the military's recruitment table at a job fair at the University of Wisconsin-Madison. A couple days before that, several dozen students chased military recruiters off campus at Southern Connecticut State University (SCSU). In September 2004, more than a hundred students protested the presence of military recruiters at the University of Pennsylvania. On February 22, 2005, several dozen students picketed recruiters at the University of Illinois campus in Chicago. At the USC Law School, recruiters were met with pickets and leafleters demanding that they leave, and at UC Berkeley, a couple dozen students protested the presence of a military recruiter table there. These are but a few of the dozens of protests that have taken place.

Meanwhile, in high schools across the US, more students and their parents seem to be opting out of taking the Armed Services Vocational Aptitude Battery (ASVAB), a test given to high school juniors as a method of targeting potential recruits. It is an admissions and placement test for the US military. All persons enlisting in the US military are required to take the ASVAB. Although the military does not usually start turning up the pressure to join the military until students reach their senior year, about 14,000 high schools nationwide give this test to juniors. A recent piece in the *Boston Globe* detailed the troubles one recruiting office in New Hampshire is facing this year. According to ASVAB testing coordinator at the Military Entrance Processing Station in Boston, which handles enlistment processing for Rhode Island, much of New Hampshire and parts of Massachusetts, many parents are writing notes excusing their kids from taking the test. At one high school in Nashua, NH, school administrators opted out of even administering the test this year. This is not an isolated case either; of the thirty schools in the Boston region that administered the test in 2004, only nineteen signed up to do so this year. One wonders how long it will be before the military makes the test mandatory for graduation.

Campus antiwar groups that formed in the past three years have called most of the university and college protests. In addition, lesbian and gay organizations and individuals have joined in because of their opposition to the military's "don't ask, don't tell" policy on homosexuality. Of course, many of the latter group also opposes the war in Iraq. According to a federal appeals court ruling made in November 2004, the essentially anti-gay policies of the military do allow universities to deny its recruiters access to their students and property. On top of that ruling, another federal judge in Connecticut found that the government unconstitutionally applied the Solomon Amendment after Yale Law School faculty sued Donald Rumsfeld when he attempted to deny federal funds to Yale because it prevented military recruitment on its campus. Yale denied the recruiters access because of their discriminatory policies against gays and lesbians.

While this strategy is not necessarily the best political strategy possible to chase recruiters off campus, it is a legal tool counter-recruitment activists should utilize while it exists. In my mind, the best political strategy is one that challenges the imperial policies of the US and calls into question not just the military's discriminatory recruitment policies, but also the role of the military itself. A strategy based on this premise would not only diminish the military's visibility, it would also challenge young people (and the rest of us) to examine for whom and what the military really fights. Additionally, it would allow the organizers of these campaigns to include defense contractors in their campaign. After all, it is these corporations that truly need young men and women to go to war.

> *"Poverty can be eradicated by loaning poor people the capital they need to engage in profitable businesses ..."*

Micro-Loans Can Be the Solution to Developing Countries' Economies

Mark Skousen

Mark Skousen is the author of many books on financial issues, including The Big Three in Economics. *In the following viewpoint, he discusses Nobel Peace Prize winner Muhammad Yunus's work with Grameen Bank, which extends micro-loans to the world's poor. The Grameen Bank makes small loans to entrepreneurs in third world countries with the intention of reducing poverty. According to Yunus, the world's poor can be pulled out of dire economic straits with the aid of compassionate investors who can teach them how to manage debt.*

As you read, consider the following questions:

1. How much interest does the Grameen Bank charge for micro-loans?

Mark Skousen, "Muhammad Yunus and the Grameen Bank: The Nobel Peace Prize-Winning Genius Behind the World's Most Original Bank (Which Is 'Giving Away' $50 Bills)," *Investment U*, October 27, 2006. Copyright © 1997–2008. Reproduced by permission.

2. How much money has the Grameen Bank made in loans?

3. How many branches does the Grameen Bank have in Bangladesh?

I remember as a young boy people telling me that borrowing money and going into debt were very, very bad.

"Neither a lender nor borrower be," declared Shakespeare. Ben Franklin warned in *The Way to Wealth*, "The first vice is running in debt . . . You give to another power over your liberty . . . Be frugal and free."

And church leader J. Rueben Clark says debt "never sleeps nor sickens nor dies . . . and whenever you get in its way or cross its course or fail to meet its demands, it crushes you."

Financial advisors warn repeatedly to stay out of debt, and gold bugs [people who invest in gold] publish charts showing the national debt by consumers, business and government climbing to unsustainable levels.

Sounds ominous, doesn't it?

Going into debt is a serious matter and should not be done lightly. I don't recommend it for most consumer goods, and certainly not for buying food at the grocery store or 7-Eleven. In short, use cash.

Debt, however, does have its advantages. In this issue, we'll discuss Nobel Peace Prize winner Muhammad Yunus, founder of the Grameen Bank and the Micro-Credit Revolution. First, a closer look at the virtue of debt as it relates to the Micro-Credit movement. . . .

The Profitable Side of Managed Debt

If handled properly, easy credit allows you and your family to buy a car or a home when you're young. Paying a monthly mortgage is a forced savings plan. After 30 years, you own the home outright. Real estate guru Jack Miller said it best: "Want to become a millionaire? Borrow a million dollars and pay it off."

And where would most businesses be without loans and credit lines from banks, investment bankers, insurance companies, mortgage companies and venture capitalists? Without these sources of capital, where would our savings go? You can't build a sophisticated complex global economy on equity financing alone. Mortgages, bridge loans, commercial and government bonds, even junk bonds are necessary to lubricate the financial world.

If you have the wherewithal to pay the interest on the debt, you can survive and even prosper, as a consumer or business—and even a government. On the other extreme, if you can't pay the interest, debt can "crush you," as Clark says. . . .

The Difference Between Starvation and Prosperity

For those of you still skeptical about the virtue of debt, consider this . . .

Laily Begun and her husband, Atiqullah, were manual laborers in Bangladesh who barely had enough to eat. She took out a $50 "micro" loan from the Grameen Bank to buy a cow, which allowed her to make some extra cash selling milk.

She borrowed another $65 for a second cow, and her little business flourished. Now she had enough to apply for a mobile phone. Laily became known as the "Village Phone Lady," and before long, she was earning nearly $300 a month. With their savings, the couple set up five shops and a restaurant. They now live in a brick house, own two color TVs, a refrigerator and a cassette player, and send their three children to school.

All because of a $50 starter loan.

The Grameen Bank is not a charity. Billions in foreign aid have been thrown at poor people without effect. Only when a for-profit bank began lending to the desperately poor did anything positive come of it. Grameen Bank charges 18% interest

Micro Loans, Solid Returns

Microfinance institutions (MFIs) . . . get capital from individual and institutional investors in the U.S. and Europe via microfinance funds. Groups that run the funds collect the money, vet the lenders, offer them management assistance, and administer investors' accounts. In the vast world of global finance, microfinance is, well, microscopic. But it is growing. The microfinance information eXchange, an industry tracking group, says its universe of 60 leading microfinance institutions lent $3.1 billion to poor borrowers in 2003, the latest available figures. That's more than twice the $1.4 billion loaned in 2000. But because the loans are small, sometimes $50 or $100, the money goes far. Microcredit Summit Campaign, another microfinance watcher, says the 779 MFIs in its database serve about 81 million customers in Latin America, Eastern Europe, Africa, and Asia. Loans are made for a variety of purposes: manufacturing, transportation, agriculture, and retailing.

BusinessWeek,
"Micro Loans, Solid Returns," May 9, 2005.

on its micro-loans, and has only a 5% default rate. How is this possible? Borrowers must join small support groups, and if one defaults, the others are forced to take over his debts.

It seems impossible, but so far the Grameen Bank has made more than $5 billion in loans, and its model has been imitated around the world, even by the World Bank.

The genius behind the Grameen Bank and the Micro-Credit Revolution is Muhammad Yunus, who just won the Nobel Peace Prize for his work with the poor. He is a former professor at the Chittagong University who decided not to just teach about the wealth of nations, but to do something about it.

Yunus founded the Grameen Bank in the world's poorest country, and today has branches in over 71,371 villages in Bangladesh through collateral-free micro credits to needy entrepreneurs.

While the World Bank has imitated his micro-credit model, Yunus decries the organization in his book *Banker to the Poor*: "We at the Grameen Bank have never wanted or accepted World Bank funding because we do not like the way the bank conducts business." Nor does he like foreign aid. "Aid-funding projects create massive bureaucracies, which quickly become corrupt and inefficient, incurring huge losses."

Yunus was a Marxist until he came to the United States and saw how the market liberates the individual. "I do believe in the power of the global free-market economy and in using capitalist tools. . . . I also believe that providing unemployment benefits is not the best way to address poverty."

Not surprisingly, the Grameen Bank is considered by Marxists as the "enemy" of the socialist revolution.

Yunus believes that poverty can be eradicated by loaning poor people the capital they need to engage in profitable businesses, not by giving them a handout or engaging in population control. In his own words, "All human beings are potential entrepreneurs."

> *"I fear that the principal effect of micro-lending is to further hook people into dependence upon the money economy."*

Micro-Loans Will Hinder Developing Countries' Economies

Josh Kearns

Josh Kearns runs Aqueous Solutions, a non-governmental organization that helps teach and promote self-reliant forms of water purification. In the following viewpoint, he argues that micro-loans like those promoted by Nobel Peace Prize winner Muhammad Yunus's Grameen Bank are not the answer to world poverty. In fact, these micro-loans only create a dependence on money among people who are already fairly self-sufficient. Kearns warns, micro-loans may do a disservice to the poor and the world's economy by increasing reliance on a money-based economy, which can collapse.

As you read, consider the following questions:

1. Why is it hard to depend on profits earned from using a micro-loan to start a business?

2. According to the author, what must all people do before they can help the poor?

3. Why are the poorest countries in the world in a better position to help Western countries than we are to help them?

I want to urge caution in what has become a widespread and unqualified enthusiasm for the whole micro-finance thing. Since [Muhammad] Yunus won the Nobel [Peace] Prize, people have been afraid to criticize the idea of micro-finance.

But I hold a great degree of skepticism about the effectiveness of micro-loans to promote authentic well-being and prosperity for folks in the so-called "developing world" over the long term. I hasten to add that I am not dismissing the concept 100%, out-of-hand. But I have serious doubts.

I fear that the principal effect of micro-lending is to further hook people into dependence upon the money economy. In the so-called "developed" world, we can scarcely imagine a thing such as independence—we are totally reliant on money to buy everything we need and want for our lives.

But the rural "poor" of the world—the subsistence farmers, for example—can and do maintain a significant degree of independence from the money economy.

They do this by producing much of what they use themselves or within their immediate communities. This kind of locally self-reliant economy is preferable—it is far more stable, more ecologically sound, and more preservative of community than the global economy.

Development for Good?

My fear is that micro-lending provides yet another mechanism (under the failed rubric of "development") for inducing folks off the land and out of their local communities, estranging them from their traditional cultures and thrusting them into the cities, which is to say the slums.

The best strategy to "help the poor" is to reduce their requirements for money, not find ways to make them more dependent upon it, even if those ways involve giving them a little money and even perhaps appear helpful in the short term.

Micro-lending involves giving the "poor" a little bit of money at the outset, which from our perspective (as rich Westerners) looks good because we can't imagine a life without money.

We think the problem of the poor is that they don't have enough money. On the contrary, their problem is lack of entitlement to the necessities of life. Money is only one way to obtain this entitlement, and it's not a very good way in the long run, neither for the world's "poor" nor ourselves.

The Trouble with Loans

A better way to secure entitlement to the necessities of life—in either the "developing" or developed worlds—is to increase local capacity for their direct creation; promoting local self-reliance.

A loan, micro- or otherwise, has to be repaid. That means an enterprise started on a micro-loan must not only be solvent, but must produce a surplus and earn sufficient profit above the interest rate of the loan.

The possibility of earning a profit is largely beyond the control of the micro-loan recipient. It is subject to the fluctuations and instabilities of the global economy and the decisions of far-flung bureaucrats in governments and international financial institutions such as the IMF [International Monetary Fund] and World Bank: all complex forces well beyond the ken [understanding], let alone the control, of a Kenyan peasant woman selling bread from an urban sidewalk stand.

If we want to "help the poor," the surest strategy is to work with them to increase their independence from the money economy. This is unfamiliar territory to nearly everyone in the West. Since we (most of us, comparatively speaking) have money, it is our stand-by solution to everything. "Throw money at the problem" is our strategy in research, public welfare programs, environmental issues and politics.

What we must do in order to be able to "help the poor" is to first learn ourselves how to live without money, or at least with a lot less of it. We must learn, or rather re-learn, the techniques of self-reliant, agrarian living wherein local needs are met primarily by goods produced locally.

I am not suggesting—God forbid—that everyone ought to "go be a farmer." We need "urban agrarians" just as desperately as rural ones.

We must familiarize ourselves with our local ecosystems and devise solutions for living that make sense within our particular ecological and social contexts. And we must re-establish the health of community that makes locally self-reliant living feasible, as it cannot be done by the individualist "loners" under the influence of "modern" society and market culture.

Breaking Control

When we consider that we must first help ourselves in these formidable tasks before helping the world's poor, we reach the ineluctable conclusion that we are, at present, woefully unqualified for the task. Our standard answer to life's problems—to spend more money—cannot produce the needed long-term solutions.

The last thing these communities need are more enticements into the money economy and the overly-consumptive modern urbanized lifestyles.

What seems ironic, though only from our own perspective, is that some of the "poorest" communities in the world are in a better position to help us than we them. Some subsistence farming communities of Asia, Africa and Latin America

What Microloans Miss

Institutional and individual investments in microfinance more than doubled between 2004 and 2006, to $4.4 billion, and the total volume of loans made has risen to $25 billion, according to Deutsche Bank. Unfortunately, it has also translated into a flood of hype. There's no doubt that microfinance does a tremendous amount of good, yet there are also real limits to what it can accomplish. Microloans make poor borrowers better off. But, on their own, they often don't do much to make poor countries richer. . . .

James Surowiecki, "What Microloans Miss"
The New Yorker, *March 17, 2008.*

still practice a lifestyle that involves a high degree of local self-reliance, strong community bonds, ecological literacy, and a well-developed sense of place.

The last thing these communities need are more enticements into the money economy and the overly-consumptive and ultimately unsatisfying modern urbanized lifestyles. To the extent that micro-lending programs draw folks further into the money economy and market culture, they create financial dependence and advance the attendant breakdown of community and destruction of ecosystems.

So as far as micro-lending tourism is concerned, I would suggest instead that travelers seek first-hand experience and insight into self-sufficient community lifestyles.

Such agrarian projects are developing worldwide, and our participation as travelers helps both to advance the communities' independence from the global economy and provides us with invaluable experiential learning possibilities that prepare us to help our own society break its addiction to globalization, growth and monetary dependence.

Periodical Bibliography

The following articles have been selected to supplement the diverse views presented in this chapter.

Stephen Armstrong   "Boutique Banking," *New Statesman*, April 20, 2009.

Choice   "Slaying the Debt Dragon," May 2009.

Jane Bennett Clark   "'I'm Buried in Debt,'" *Kiplinger's Personal Finance*, May 2009.

Cora Daniels   "Smart Money Moves," *Essence*, April 2009.

Niall Ferguson   "Diminished Returns," *The New York Times Magazine*, May 17, 2009.

Dan Kadlec   "They Paid You Well to Get Out. Now What?" *Money*, March 2009.

Beth Kobliner   "Help Your Kids Graduate from Debt," *Money*, April 2009.

Jennifer Lee Johnson   "Bleakonomics," *Bust*, April/May 2009.

Simon Johnson   "The Quiet Coup," *Atlantic Monthly*, May 2009.

David Malpass   "Ranking the Devils: Debt, Deficits, Dollar Weakness," *Forbes*, April 27, 2009.

Mike Murphy   "The Sacrifice Gap," *Time*, May 25, 2009.

The New York Times Magazine   "Banks of America," March 15, 2009.

Christopher Palmeri   "Take a Haircut Now, Avoid Bankruptcy?" *BusinessWeek*, May 4, 2009.

Richard Thaler   "It Doesn't Have to Hurt," *Newsweek*, April 20, 2009.

Kai Wright   "More Mortgage Madness," *Nation*, May 19, 2009.

For Further Discussion

Chapter 1

1. Tom Allen argues that going into debt can be beneficial, while Mark Johannessen of the Financial Planning Association argues that debt is never a good option. After reading each viewpoint, do you think going into debt can be helpful? How does each viewpoint influence your understanding of the issue?

2. Leslie E. Royale and *USA Today (Magazine)* debate whether it is possible to live entirely debt free. Based on the evidence each provides, do you think living debt free is plausible? Why or why not?

3. Michelle Singletary and Brian Alderson debate about the kind of relationship that should exist between debtors and creditors. Which viewpoint offers the most persuasive argument? Explain your answer.

Chapter 2

1. Jonathan Burton argues that teens should be given credit cards, while Carolyn M. Brown argues that they should not. Which viewpoint is more convincing? Why?

2. Sandra Guy and Bob Ellis debate about whether women or men have a harder time managing debt. Which viewpoint offers the most persuasive argument? Explain your answer.

Chapter 3

1. What evidence does Steven Lachance give to support his argument that the U.S. economy is failing because it is debt-based? What evidence does Andrew Leonard give to

support his argument that the U.S. economy is failing because it is credit-based? Whose viewpoint do you find most convincing and why?

2. Nathalie Martin argues that the U.S. government should encourage consumers to take on more credit in order to help the economy. Shepherd Bliss argues the opposite. After reading the two viewpoints, do you think consumer debt is a way to encourage economic growth?

3. Saul Kanowitz argues that the United States exploits developing nations by lending them money that they know these poor nations will never be able to repay. J.R. Dieckmann argues that the United States has created its own crisis by loaning too much money to poorer countries. Based on the evidence offered, should the United States loan money to other nations?

Chapter 4

1. What evidence does Laura Cohn use to argue that filing bankruptcy can help families start over? What evidence does Alison Smith-Squire use to argue that filing bankruptcy can tear families apart? Whose viewpoint is most convincing and why?

2. Janet Kidd Stewar and Ron Jacobs debate the helpfulness of joining the military to pay for a college education. Based on the evidence offered, do you think enlisting is an effective way to pay for higher education?

3. Mark Skousen argues that micro-loans can help build the economies of struggling countries. Based on the evidence he provides, can you imagine circumstances in which this strategy might work? Or do you agree with Josh Kearns who asserts that not only do micro-loans not help developing economies, they might actually harm them?

Organizations to Contact

The editors have compiled the following list of organizations concerned with the issues debated in this book. The descriptions are derived from materials provided by the organizations. All have publications or information available for interested readers. The list was compiled on the date of publication of the present volume; the information provided here may change. Be aware that many organizations take several weeks or longer to respond to inquiries, so allow as much time as possible.

Americans for Fairness in Lending (AFFIL)

7 Winthrop Square, 4th Floor, Boston, MA 02110
(617) 841-8000
e-mail: info@affil.org
Web site: www.affil.org

Americans for Fairness in Lending (AFFIL) is working to reform the lending industry to protect Americans' financial assets. They work to educate and advocate for American consumers and small businesses. In addition to a regularly updated blog, AFFIL's Web site offers statements about lending practices, including "Credit Card Law's Effect on People Under 21" and "A New Era for Credit Cards."

Center for Responsible Lending (CRL)

302 West Main Street, Durham, NC 27701
(919) 313-8500
Web site: www.responsiblelending.org

The Center for Responsible Lending (CRL) is a nonprofit, nonpartisan research and policy organization dedicated to protecting homeownership and family wealth by working to eliminate abusive financial practices. CRL has conducted and commissioned landmark studies on predatory lending practices and the impact of state laws that protect borrowers. They also publish many resources for consumers, including fact sheets on payday loans, overdraft loans, and mortgages.

Consumer Action (CA)

221 Main Street, Suite 480, San Francisco, CA 94105
(415) 777-9635 • fax: (415) 777-5267
Web site: www.consumer-action.org

Consumer Action (CA) is a nonprofit, membership-based organization that was founded in San Francisco in 1971. During its more than three decades, Consumer Action has continued to serve consumers nationwide by advancing consumer rights and publishing educational materials in multiple languages. Among their many publications, several focus on debt, such as "Debt Consolidation: Is It for You?" and "Families and Credit Cards."

Consumer Federation of America (CFA)

1620 I Street NW, Suite 200, Washington, DC 20006
(202) 387-6121
e-mail: cfa@consumerfed.org
Web site: www.consumerfed.org

Since 1968, Consumer Federation of America's (CFA's) professional staff has gathered facts, analyzed issues, and disseminated information to the public, policy makers, and the rest of the consumer movement. The size and diversity of its membership—approximately 280 nonprofit organizations from throughout the nation with a combined membership exceeding 50 million people—enables CFA to speak for virtually all consumers. In addition to original studies, the CFA regularly publishes brochures and fact sheets available free to the public, including "Building Wealth Not Debt" and "Managing Your Debts."

Consumer Watchdog (CWD)
1750 Ocean Park Boulevard, Suite 200
Santa Monica, CA   90405
(310) 392-0522 • fax: (310) 392-8874
e-mail: admin@consumerwatchdog.org
Web site: www.consumerwatchdog.org

Consumer Watchdog (CWD) (formerly the Foundation for Taxpayer and Consumer Rights) is a nationally recognized consumer group that has been fighting corrupt corporations and politicians since 1985. Over the years, Consumer Watchdog has worked to save Americans billions of dollars by speaking out on behalf of patients, ratepayers, and policyholders. In addition to serving as a clearinghouse of financial information, CWD publishes books regarding consumer advocacy, including *Corporateering: How Corporate Power Steals Your Personal Freedom*.

Consumers Union (CU)
101 Truman Avenue, Yonkers, NY   10703-1057
(914) 378-2000
Web site: www.consumersunion.org

Consumers Union (CU) is an independent, nonprofit organization dedicated to working for a fair, just, and safe marketplace for all consumers. The organization strives to change legislation and the marketplace to favor the consumer interest and several public education Web sites. CU publishes *Consumer Reports* and two newsletters, *Consumer Reports on Health* and *Consumer Reports Money Advisor*.

Federal Trade Commission (FTC)
600 Pennsylvania Avenue NW, Washington, DC   20580
(877) 382-4357 (FTC-HELP)
Web site: www.ftc.gov

Founded in 1914, the Federal Trade Commission (FTC) pursues vigorous and effective law enforcement and creates practical and plain-language educational programs for consumers and businesses. The FTC also administers a wide variety of consumer protection laws, including the Telemarketing Sales Rule, the Pay-Per-Call Rule and the Equal Credit Opportunity Act. In addition to an annual "Performance and Accountability Report," the FTC regularly publishes consumer protection materials, including "Credit and Your Consumer Rights" and "Knee Deep in Debt."

National Association of Consumer Advocates (NACA)
1730 Rhode Island Avenue NW, Suite 710
Washington, DC   20036
(202) 452-1989 • fax: (202) 452-0099
e-mail: info@naca.net
Web site: www.naca.net

The National Association of Consumer Advocates (NACA) is a nationwide organization of more than 1,500 members who represent and have represented hundreds of thousands of consumers victimized by fraudulent, abusive and predatory business practices. NACA's members and their clients are actively engaged in promoting a fair and open marketplace that forcefully protects the rights of consumers, particularly those of modest means. The NACA's Web site serves as a clearinghouse of information about predatory lending practices, debt collection abuse, and credit reporting problems.

Truth About Credit
44 Winter Street, Boston, MA   02108
(617) 747-4330
Web site: www.truthaboutcredit.org

Truth About Credit is a project of the U.S. Public Education Fund and the Student PIRGs (Public Interest Research Groups). Both organizations conduct research, education, and advocacy on behalf of consumers. To protect student consumers, the Truth About Credit project aims to reduce students' exposure to the worst credit practices that trap them into unfair terms and conditions. Some of their most recent publications include "The Campus Credit Card Trap" and "Characteristics of Fair Campus Credit Cards."

U.S. Department of the Treasury

1500 Pennsylvania Avenue NW, Washington, DC 20220
(202) 622-2000 • fax: (202) 622-6415
Web site: www.ustreas.gov

The U.S. Department of the Treasury is the executive agency responsible for promoting economic prosperity and ensuring the financial security of the United States. The Department is responsible for a wide range of activities such as advising the president on economic and financial issues, encouraging sustainable economic growth, and fostering improved governance in financial institutions. In addition to fact sheets and press releases, the Treasury's Web site includes many publications such as "Protecting American Credit Card Holders" and "Regulations for the Credit Reporting Industry."

Bibliography of Books

Sumit Agarwal, Chunlin Liu, and Nicholas S. Souleles
The Reaction of Consumer Spending and Debt to Tax Rebates: Evidence from Consumer Credit Data. Cambridge, MA: National Bureau of Economic Research, 2007.

Curtis E. Arnold
How You Can Profit from Credit Cards: Using Credit to Improve Your Financial Life and Bottom Line. Upper Saddle River, NJ: FT Press, 2008.

Karen Bellenir, ed.
Debt Information for Teens. Detroit, MI: Omnigraphics, 2008.

Patrick Bolton, Xavier Freixas, and Joel Shapiro
The Credit Ratings Game. Cambridge, MA: National Bureau of Economic Research, 2009.

William Bonner and Addison Wiggin
Empire of Debt: The Rise of an Epic Financial Crisis. Hoboken, NJ: Wiley, 2006.

Russell J. Bruemmer and Andrew L. Sandler
Subprime Credit Crisis: Everything You Need to Know Now. New York: Practicing Law Institute, 2008.

Warren Brussee
The Great Depression of Debt: Survival Techniques for Every Investor. Hoboken, NJ: John Wiley and Sons, 2009.

Hess Chung and Eric M. Leeper
What Has Financed Government Debt? Cambridge, MA: National Bureau of Economic Research, 2007.

A. Geske Dijkstra — *The Impact of International Debt Relief.* New York: Routledge, 2008.

Simeon Djankov — *Debt Enforcement Around the World.* Cambridge, MA: National Bureau of Economic Research, 2006.

Jochen Felsenheimer and Philip Gisdakis — *Credit Crises: From Tainted Loans to a Global Economic Meltdown.* Weinheim: Wiley-VCH, 2008.

Mary Hunt — *Debt Proof Your Kids.* Los Angeles, CA: DPL Press, 2006.

Margaret C. Jasper — *Dealing with Debt.* Dobbs Ferry, NY: Oceana Publications, 2007.

Anya Kamenetz — *Generation Debt: Why Now Is a Terrible Time to Be Young.* New York: Riverhead Books/Penguin, 2006.

Lynnette Khalfani — *Zero Debt for College Grads: From Student Loans to Financial Freedom.* New York: Kaplan Publishing, 2007.

Herwig M. Langohr and Patricia T. Langohr — *The Rating Agencies and Their Credit Ratings: What They Are, How They Work, and Why They Are Relevant.* Hoboken, NJ: John Wiley, 2008.

Annamaria Lusardi and Peter Tufano — *Debt Literacy, Financial Experiences, and Overindebtedness.* Cambridge, MA: National Bureau of Economic Research, 2009.

Enrique G. Mendoza — *Lessons from the Debt-Deflation Theory of Sudden Stops.* Cambridge, MA: National Bureau of Economic Research, 2006.

Michael Mihalik — *Debt Is Slavery: And Nine Other Things I Wish My Dad Had Taught Me About Money.* Seattle: October Mist Publishing, 2007.

Reinhard Neck and Jan-Egbert Sturm, eds. — *Sustainability of Public Debt.* Cambridge, MA: MIT Press, 2008.

Ann Pettifor — *The Coming First World Debt Crisis.* New York: Palgrave Macmillan, 2006.

Carmen M. Reinhart and Kenneth S. Rogoff — *The Forgotten History of Domestic Debt.* Cambridge, MA: National Bureau of Economic Research, 2008.

Jason R. Rich — *Smart Debt.* Irvine, CA: Entrepreneur Press, 2007.

Matt Schoenfeld — *Living Debt Free: Principles for Abundant Living.* Kansas City, MO: Beacon Hill Press, 2008.

Andrew Simms — *Ecological Debt: Global Warming and the Wealth of Nations.* New York, NY: Pluto Press, 2009.

Federico Sturzenegger and Jeromin Zettelmeyer — *Debt Defaults and Lessons from a Decade of Crises.* Cambridge, MA: MIT Press, 2006.

Graham Turner — *The Credit Crunch: Housing Bubbles, Globalisation and the Worldwide Economic Crisis.* Ann Arbor, MI: Pluto Press, 2008.

Steve Weisman — *The Truth About Avoiding Credit Scams: The Essential Truths in 20 Minutes.* Upper Saddle River, NJ: FT Press, 2009.

Liz Pulliam Weston — *Deal with Your Debt: The Right Way to Manage Your Bills and Pay Off What You Owe.* Upper Saddle River, NJ: Pearson Prentice Hall, 2006.

Robert E. Wright — *One Nation Under Debt: Hamilton, Jefferson, and the History of What We Owe.* New York: McGraw-Hill, 2008.

Index